IMAGES OI

ALLIED POWs IN GERMAN HANDS 1914-1918

RARE PHOTOGRAPHS FROM WARTIME ARCHIVES

David Bilton

Pen & Sword
MILITARY

First published in Great Britain in 2016 by
PEN & SWORD MILITARY
An imprint of
Pen & Sword Books Ltd
47 Church Street
Barnsley
South Yorkshire
S70 2AS

ISBN 978-1-47386-701-7

Typeset by Concept, Huddersfield, West Yorkshire HD4 5JL.
Printed and bound in England by CPI Group (UK) Ltd, Croydon CR0 4YY.

Pen & Sword Books Ltd incorporates the imprints of Pen & Sword Archaeology, Atlas, Aviation, Battleground, Discovery, Family History, History, Maritime, Military, Naval, Politics, Railways, Select, Social History, Transport, True Crime, and Claymore Press, Frontline Books, Leo Cooper, Praetorian Press, Remember When, Seaforth Publishing and Wharncliffe.

For a complete list of Pen & Sword titles please contact
PEN & SWORD BOOKS LIMITED
47 Church Street, Barnsley, South Yorkshire S70 2AS, England
E-mail: enquiries@pen-and-sword.co.uk
Website: www.pen-and-sword.co.uk

Contents

Acknowledgements

As with previous books, a great big thank you to the staff of the Prince Consort's Library for their help, kindness and knowledge during the pre-writing stages of this book. While some of the pictures come from books mentioned in the bibliography, the remainder are from a private collection.

Die große Schlacht im Westen.
An der Strasse nach Peronne rastende gefangene Engländer.

The utter exhaustion of fighting and capture is clearly shown in this photograph taken during the Somme Offensive in 1916. 'The great battle in the west. English prisoners resting on the road to Peronne.'

Preface

During the war the German authorities published a photographic account of PoW life in a German prison camp. Although issued ostensibly by the Librairie de l'Université Otto Gschwand in Fribourg, Switzerland it was printed in Germany in three languages, German, French and English. After the war, as part of the Armistice and Peace treaties, Germany published a book showing that it had not mistreated the prisoners and that any harm that befell them was their own responsibility.

A number of the illustrations from these books have been used in this book. What is interesting about those who bought photos as souvenirs is that most of them appear to have been French. As most Russians were poor that is probably the reason why there are so few private Russian cards, but there are also comparatively few British cards. Interestingly, in the German official pictures there are very few British present: most are photos of happy French and Russian prisoners.

Looking at the private purchase photographs kept by the inmates of the various prisons and reading the post-war testimony of the men held captive, few bear witness to the contents of either of these books. Neither show the appalling conditions recorded by some of the men. There are few if any photographs of the men working in the salt mines and other dangerous places. In general the men look fit, often quite happy and remarkably healthy. This contradicts the personal accounts. Which is true? Or are both true? Was it not as awful an experience for some as it was for others? Were some lucky and others not? While comparing the pictures with the text, readers will no doubt make up their own mind.

Introduction

The concept of the prisoner of war is a relatively new idea. At the end of a battle, there had always been the dead and those that survived. What happened to the survivors depended on whether they had won or lost, who they were fighting and their position in society.

Throughout history wars have produced prisoners, men whose life was at the whim of the victor. What could be expected has changed through the centuries, but even with rules the position of the prisoner has never been secure. Even with the Geneva Conventions, a set of rules of conduct for warfare, security is not guaranteed, especially as not every country signed the conventions and many who did, only paid them lip service. Prior to 1931 there was no convention for prisoners, only regulations on the treatment of sick and wounded soldiers.

How have prisoners fared? Soldiers captured by the Ancient Greeks or Romans could end up as slaves but later become freemen, while those taken by the Aztecs were usually ritually sacrificed. In Japan, which had custom of ransom, prisoners were for the most part summarily executed. The rich could look forward to ransom but for most it was not an option. In early times the same fate awaited many who were non-combatants, merely citizens of the defeated nation. Religious wars were generally bloody affairs as it was felt better to kill the heretic. While the freeing of prisoners was a charitable act in Islam, Muslim scholars believed the leader of the Muslim force capturing non-Muslims could choose to kill, ransom or enslave them, or cut off their hands and feet on alternate sides. Fortunately, as warfare changed, so did the treatment of captives and the general population.

During the Middle Ages enslavement of enemy soldiers declined but ransoming was widespread and continued into the seventeenth century. For practical and ethical reasons, fewer civilians were taken prisoner: they were extra mouths to feed; and it was considered neither just nor necessary. 'The development of the use of the mercenary soldier also tended to create a slightly more tolerant climate for a prisoner, for the victor in one battle knew that he might be the vanquished in the next.'[1]

Enlightened thought during the sixteenth and seventeenth centuries proposed that 'in war no destruction of life or property beyond that necessary to decide the conflict'[2] was necessary. During the same period the widespread enslavement of prisoners came to an end with the Treaty of Westphalia in 1648 which released prisoners without ransom. The idea of parole developed during the period. This was only allowable for officers because their word could be trusted. In exchange for

Franzosen		Russen		Belgier		Engländ·	
Mannschaften	Offiz.	Mannschaften	Offiz.	Mannsch	Offiz.	Mannsch	Off.
215 905	3452 7 General	300 294	3557 18 General	36852	609 3 Gen	18824	492
219 364		309 869		37464		19316	

German propaganda – boasting of the number of PoWs held in less than five months of war.

swearing not to escape they received better accommodation and greater freedom, and for those who swore not to take up arms again against the captor nation they could be repatriated or exchanged.

During the eighteenth century a new attitude of morality in the law of nations, or international law, had a profound effect upon the problem of prisoners of war. The writings of Montesquieu, Rousseau and de Vattel were to help improve the treatment of prisoners: a captor's only right over a prisoner was to prevent him doing harm, and they could be quarantined to prevent them returning to the fight. These ideas were not always adhered to and during the American War of Independence captured Americans were classified as criminals; no longer protected as PoWs, they could be treated differently. Many thousands died from starvation and exposure in crowded prison ships off the coast. Twenty years later the first purpose-built PoW camp was established at Norman Cross to house French prisoners from the French

(*Left*) Casualty lists appearing in newspapers across the country detailed the cost of the war to towns and cities. This is part of the casualty list for the Reading area in May 1915. Many of those who were posted missing were dead but some were PoWs. The lack of information was especially distressing as it could be many months, indeed years, before the facts were known.

(*Right*) From missing, a man could progress to being unofficially reported as a PoW, but for some it was never official. This is the newspaper listing for J. Wheel who was aboard HMS *Turbulent* when it was sunk by SMS *Westfalen* in the battle of Jutland.

The original caption was *Lustige Gesellschaft – Garçons gais – Jolly fellows*. They are all French.

For those waiting at home the arrival of such a postcard was the most wonderful thing ever. A postcard from Seaman Wheel, nearly a month after the battle, informing his sister that he was still alive. Written on 4 July it was not franked for delivery until 17 July; how long it took to get to England is not known. On the back of the card he told his sister he was well. 'I expect you have been thinking about me when you saw the paper but I am pleased to say that I all right (sic.), would you be so good as to send me a parcle (sic.) of food which would come in very exceptable (sic.), we are having very hot weather just now & things are not very good … remember me to all at home …'

Revolutionary and Napoleonic wars. The prison was intended as a model prison, providing the most humane treatment possible to thousands of men. Food rations were as good as the food eaten by the local population.

During both the American Civil War and the Franco-Prussian War there were clear principles for the treatment of prisoners, but their observance left much to be desired. As a result, international conferences in 1899 and 1907 at The Hague drew up rules of conduct for the treatment of PoWs and incorporated the provisions of the Geneva Convention of 1864. This gave guidance as to the treatment of the wounded and forbade the killing of enemy combatants who had surrendered. This had been ratified by Germany and other nations and was further ratified with minor changes in 1907. Chapter II provided strict guidelines on the rights of PoWs: they were in the power of the hostile government, not those who captured them or their commanders; their treatment was to be humane; and all their personal belongings remained theirs (this naturally did not include their arms, horses or military papers).

As a result of these two conventions, soldiers captured in the Great War were provided some protection, but with PoWs numbering in their millions, inevitably there would be infractions. After the war there were many charges that the rules had not been followed and in May–July 1921 war crime trials were held. Only twelve men were indicted, seven for mistreating prisoners. Four were found guilty and sentenced to prison terms ranging from a few months to two years. The leniency of the court was seen by those outside Germany as a travesty; in Germany the punishment was felt to be excessively harsh. In 1929 there was a further Geneva Convention that would regulate PoW treatment in the next war.

Notes

1. Britannia.com. Prisoner of war.
2. Ibid.

Chapter One

Capture

Surrender and capture were essentially unknowns to the fighting soldier. A brave heroic death was shown as the way to fight, encapsulated by the Latin phrase – or 'old lie' depending on your view – *dulce et decorum est pro patria mori*. While many might wish for a Blighty wound that would take them out of the war, being taken prisoner was another thing. A genuine injury or death were honourable things; surrender was at best suspicious, at worst cowardice.

At school, history lessons were about victory, not surrender. Regimental traditions reinforced honour and notions of what was right and proper. No soldier wanted to bring dishonour to their regiment, and of course you had to stand true to your pals and comrades. If you surrendered, there was guilt to contend with. Second Lieutenant Crowder of 256 Brigade RFA was taken prisoner on 21 March 1918. He remembered feeling that he 'had let the side down. For days afterwards I was worrying about what I could have done.'[1]

Then there was the official attitude. It did not officially disapprove of surrender, but merely suggested that it might not be the best move to make. German propaganda reported the brutality of Allied camps to encourage their soldiers not to surrender but fight to the death. While the British did not encourage fighting to the end unless ordered, they claimed that in Germany, Allied prisoners were systematically persecuted by order of the German government. The fact that any captured British officer had to explain the reasons for his capture in a written report may have affected the decision of many – they were not to know that they would be exonerated after the war.

This alleged poor treatment was used as an incentive for recruiting. In mid-April 1915, Lord Nunburnholme urged the men of Hull to enlist to replace the losses the local territorial battalion were sure to incur during the coming fighting; they had recently arrived in France and were about to go into battle for the first time. 'There is urgent need of you. Come out, and avenge the terrible and inhumane treatment of British prisoners and you will look back with pride in years to come on the step you will, I am confident, take. GOD SAVE THE KING.'[2]

With the German offensive in March 1918, the official position about surrender was clearly stated. This is Haig's famous order of 11 April:

General Headquarters
Tuesday, April 11th, 1918

Three weeks ago to-day the enemy began his terrific attacks against us on a 50-mile front. His objects are to separate us from the French, to take the Channel Ports and destroy the British Army.

In spite of throwing already 106 Divisions into the battle and enduring the most reckless sacrifice of human life, he has as yet made little progress towards his goals.

We owe this to the determined fighting and self-sacrifice of our troops. Words fail me to express the admiration which I feel for the splendid resistance offered by all ranks of our Army under the most trying circumstances.

Many amongst us now are tired. To those I would say that Victory will belong to the side which holds out the longest. The French Army is moving rapidly and in great force to our support.

There is no other course open to us but to fight it out. Every position must be held to the last man: there must be no retirement. With our backs to the wall and believing in the justice of our cause each one of us must fight on to the end. The safety of our homes and the Freedom of mankind alike depend upon the conduct of each one of us at this critical moment.

(Signed) D. Haig F.M.
Commander-in-Chief
British Armies in France[3]

Obviously not everyone took note of this order. During the war, some 7,335 officers and 174,491 other ranks of the British Army were captured, with half being taken into captivity between 21 March and 11 November 1918.

The reasons for surrendering were many, often complex and individual – each man had their breaking point and individual agenda for survival. Each potential prisoner usually had only a short period in which to decide to fight, flee or give up. It is possible to summarise the main reasons for capitulation on a personal or group level:

1. Incapacitating wounds.
2. Exhaustion.
3. Orders.
4. A trench raid where a prisoner was taken.
5. Desertion to the enemy.
6. Inability to continue resistance due to shortage of ammunition, food, water.
7. Being surrounded or isolated by the enemy making a fighting retreat impossible.
8. War weariness and an unwillingness to continue fighting for a lost cause.
9. Mental collapse caused by stress – 'shell-shock'.

Regardless of the reason, the transition from combatant to prisoner has always been precarious. With heightened senses, adrenalin flowing rapidly and blood pumping quickly, men under the 'red mist' are not always in control of their more basic instincts. Why should you accept the surrender of a man who has just killed your friend? If a machine gunner stops shooting and puts his hands up just as you reach his position after mowing down half your platoon, why should he live and your platoon not? Then there is of course simple hatred or revenge for being on the receiving end of machine guns and artillery for days. There may have also been unwritten orders not to take prisoners.

The capricious nature of survival after surrender is clearly illustrated by Thomas Penrose Marks in *The Laughter Goes from Life*. Waking to shouting, Penrose's friend Bill was calling out that there was a German coming in. He lay in the dark and waited. When the enemy soldier was just yards away he stopped with one hand up and the other pointing down at the ground. '*Kamerad – pistolet!*' Fortunately for the German, Bill was right behind him so he did not shoot because the bullet might have gone through the enemy and hit his friend. Standing up he pointed his rifle and bayonet at the German. It was obvious he was surrendering. Marks wrote, 'I had no wish to take a prisoner, he just gave himself up and I could not refuse to take him. If Bill had not been directly behind him, perhaps I should not have done so. He was just plain lucky. Thus does life at the Front sometimes depend upon purely fortuitous circumstances.'[4] The three men sat down and had a cigarette.

Cigarettes played a part in the capture of Jack Rogers on 21 March 1918, his 24th birthday, when he should have been at home on leave. The Germans worked their way round both flanks and suddenly appeared behind them. Realising their situation was hopeless they all threw their guns away. Suddenly a German rushed at him, bayonet fixed, shouting in German. Jack expected to be bayoneted, but the German suddenly stopped, 'stood his gun down, looked at him and said, "*Zigaretten, Kamerad?*"'[5]

An essential part of warfare is the reduction of the enemy's manpower. Taking prisoners was clearly a good way to achieve this, more effective than wounding but not as efficient as death. The latter, preferred method of reduction, required no supervision, little space and no food, so the above descriptions can be applied to both sides, even though forbidden under the Geneva Convention. Private Taylor of the 2nd Wiltshires experienced this first-hand on 21 March 1918. 'We were stood there with our hands up and a German who told us he had been a waiter in Manchester said, "You'll be all right, boys, plenty of grub where you're going to."'[6]

The Convention clearly stated that surrendered prisoners could not be killed, but it did happen. Private Taylor told his captor 'about the wounded down one of the dugouts. He took a stick grenade out, pulled the pin and threw it down the dugout. We heard the shrieks and were nauseated, but we were completely powerless. But it was all a *mêlée* and we might have done the same in the circumstances.'[7] After all, war is war. It turned out that Taylor's unit had caused considerably more casualties among the attackers than the Germans had on them.

A private in the Norfolk Regiment, captured in October 1914, told Captain Nobbs about the murder of a prisoner. He told him that he 'had just bandaged up the leg of a man in the Cheshire Regiment, who had half his foot blown off, when all the prisoners were ordered to the rear. A German officer came up and ordered us both to get back; but I pointed out that the Cheshire man was too badly wounded to be moved without help. He ordered me to undo the bandage, and when he saw the condition of the wound, he drew his revolver and shot him dead. He then ordered me to get back.'[8]

A few days after taking the German prisoner, Marks was sipping his rum ration waiting to go over the top for the third time in forty-eight hours. They had suffered heavy casualties over the previous days and were not in the best of moods as they had expected to be relieved and rested. Suddenly a message was passed down the trench five minutes before jump-off. 'No prisoners today'.[9] The reason was simple. Losses had been high previously and there was no one spare to escort them back.

Marks explained what happened to machine gunners who stopped firing. After leaving the trench they came under heavy machine gun fire. Losing four men, they zig-zagged at the Germans who continued firing and hit another two men. When Marks' men were only 20 yards away the Germans ceased firing and threw up their hands. Standing in a shallow trench with two machine guns on the parapet with used ammunition all around and a half-used belt in one gun, eight Germans awaited their fate as five enemy soldiers charged at them. Their fate had been sealed by their actions. 'We do not even consult together to decide what to do. It is understood perfectly what we shall do. We shall just give them a dose of the medicine which they have meted out to our comrades. We shall not spare a single one of these Boches. They stand before us, and seem to know that we have taken on the role of executioners. Two or three of them call out – "*Kamerad! Kamerad!*" They are defenceless, but they have chosen to . . . I raise my rifle to the shoulder. He is only 8 yards from me. He does not move, but squeals like a kitten . . . as a last resort, he calls "*Kamerad!*" I press the trigger and fire. It is quite impossible to miss at such short range. He gives one piercing shriek, jumps clean off the ground, then crumples up . . . His seven companions are treated in the same way. They lie beside their machine guns. We survey our handiwork with satisfaction, and do not feel any sense of pity for the dead Jerries.'[10]

Lack of pity was not just something shown by the British soldier. *The Times History of the War* reported that the evidence of German brutality at the moment of capture was 'both large and weighty'.[11] According to the paper there were cases 'where British wounded, having been left in a trench, were found, on its subsequent recapture, with their throats cut'.[12]

When payback for their painful existence was on men's minds, few prisoners would be taken. After days of being machine gunned and shelled by artillery, revenge was a priority, as Marks described. At the mouth of a dugout he and his men waited for the Germans to come out. To speed the process up, a hand grenade was thrown in. The first German climbed up with hands above his head with his back to them. After twelve paces he was shot. A second emerged, screamed on seeing his comrade and was also shot. They took it in turns to shoot each one, confident that if the boot was on the other foot the same would happen.

A diary was quoted as official evidence of similar barbarity by the Germans. On 19 December 1914, an officer of *13 Regiment (Infanterie-Regiment Herwarth von Bittenfeld (1. Westfälisches Nr. 13), 13th Division, VII Armee Korps)* wrote, 'the sight of the trenches and the fury – not to say the bestiality – of our men in beating to death the wounded British affected me so much that for the rest of the day I was fit for nothing.'[13]

Every situation was different, as Private Jim Brady of the 43rd Field Ambulance recalled. He was in a dugout playing cards and stood to win with an unbeatable hand when a bullet hit the floor near his feet. Looking up, there were two Germans gazing down at them. 'One shouted, "Come up, Tommy! *Los! Los!*" And he shot another bullet, splat, into the side of the stairway.'[14] Filing upstairs, hands above heads, scared stiff, they hoped they would be recognised as non-combatants. British troops in the reserve trench spotted the Germans and opened fire. One of the RAMC men was hit. As Brady bent down to attend to him he was thumped in the ribs by a rifle butt.

In another dugout, Rifleman Burt Eccles of the 7th Rifle Brigade was sitting on the bottom step when a hand grenade was thrown down the other entrance. He rushed up with his rifle to find himself covered by at least fifty Germans. The others followed him up. One of the men was bayoneted, but the arrival of a German officer changed the situation. He wanted to question Eccles, who was a signaller. This, he felt, saved his life.

Corporal Gale, also of the 7th Rifle Brigade, had a different experience. They had just got a brew going when the Captain popped his head in the dugout door and said calmly, 'You can all come up. You won't want your rifles.'[15] They obeyed to find themselves surrounded by Germans. They were all gathered on the road when a nearby German started firing at them with a machine gun. The arrival of an officer stopped the shooting before anyone was killed.

Lance Corporal Lambert of the 7th Sherwood Foresters and Lieutenant Scott of the 6th Somerset light Infantry were also fortunate. Lambert and his squad threw off their equipment and walked up the dugout stairs when a German shouted down to them. They had heard tales of grenades and ammonal being thrown down and did not want to take the chance. They were gathered in a sunken road and an officer pointed to the rear and left them to it. He felt they had been treated fairly, after all 'that chap at the top of the dug-out could have stuck a bayonet in us as we came out.'[16] Scott's experience with a bayonet-wielding German was brief. He walked round a traverse to find a 'horrible little German with thick glasses on ... he put his bayonet at the centre of my stomach and said "*Kamerad*, yes or no?" I said, "Yes".'[17]

While most men surrendered because they wanted to live, some were ordered, regardless of what they wanted. It was a difficult decision for an officer to make: to surrender, or to continue fighting and watch your men die, possibly for no useful purpose, especially if surrounded and the battle has moved on. On 21 March 1918, Lieutenant Colonel Lord Farnham, CO 2nd Royal Inniskilling Fusiliers, took that difficult decision. His battalion were holding Boadicea Redoubt and as the day drew on it was obvious their holding the position was not delaying the German advance. German records indicate that, surrounded by overwhelming forces, they were offered the choice of surrender or destruction by heavy artillery bombardment. Lord Farnham, having received a document stating that he had put up a good fight before surrendering, duly surrendered. Farnham, carrying a small white dog, accompanied by three captains, seven subalterns and 241 other ranks, filed out of the redoubt leaving behind forty-one machine guns and mortars.

Rifleman Hall, 12th London Regiment, was cut off during a counter-attack in the Salient in May 1915. At some time during the advance he had been wounded and lost consciousness. The battalion withdrew and he was left behind. In a state of confusion, when he woke he ran towards two French soldiers he saw near a stream. Realising too late that they were in field-grey and not Horizon blue, he suddenly found himself a captive. Fortunately they escorted him towards the rear. He was lucky. Shortly after his capture, he witnessed the shooting dead of a British prisoner, Skinner, for nothing worse than insolence.

After a particularly bloody encounter in August 1914, a private in the Leicestershire Regiment had a very rough time from the men he had just been fighting against. The soldiers detailed to look after the prisoners made them run the gauntlet one by one. He and most of the men ended up very bruised but 'one chap when he was running the gauntlet was struck in the face by the butt of a rifle; his nose was smashed and his face covered in blood, and he fell to the ground insensible. They threw him into a ditch, because they thought he was dead; but he was able to crawl out next morning.'[18]

How did they feel? Ernie Stevens of the Middlesex Regiment, captured on 9 April 1918 after just one day in the trenches, recalled eighty years later what it felt like. 'That feeling of being taken prisoner was one of the worst you could ever have in your life. It was the most horrible thing I'd ever imagined could happen to me. It made me feel as if I was a coward. I was letting my country down, I was letting my unit down, I was letting my family down. A horrible, horrible feeling. I felt utterly bewildered; nothing ever occurred to me that could give me that kind of feeling, before or since, nothing. I was nearly sick thinking about it. Being taken prisoner, oh what a disgrace!'[19]

With hands in the air, the surrendering soldier no longer had any control. His life was on a thread, but once accepted as a prisoner, his chances of survival improved. However, it was not guaranteed, and even when they moved out of the battle area many still died or were killed. The number of missing PoWs was considerable. Brigadier Sir James Edmonds in *The Occupation of the Rhineland*, published in 1944, recorded that on 9 January 1919 there was a discrepancy of over 22,000 in the count of prisoners. The Germans insisted they only held 13,579 men but British records stated that there were about 36,000 still in their hands.

A diary entry from Rifleman Hall, 12th London Regiment, helps explain the difference. '580 men left Giessen on January 14th 1917 for work behind the German lines, 260 returned, of the remainder 192 died of starvation, and brutality or were shot in cold blood, 128 were admitted to hospital on their return to camp, since when many have died.'[20] On another occasion he saw a French party return after a day of hard work. One of the men had trouble keeping up and eventually fell and could not rise. 'One of the guards kicked him and hit him with his rifle, whereupon this Frenchman endeavoured to point out that he could not walk. Without more ado the Hun shot him through the heart where he lay. The next morning his comrades saw his dried blood but the body had been taken away.'[21]

Notes

1. Middlebrook, M., *The Kaiser's Battle*, Allen Lane, 1978.
2. *Hull Daily Mail*.
3. www.firstworldwar.com/source/backstothewall.htm
4. Marks, T.P., *The Laughter Goes from Life*, William Kimber, 1977.
5. MacDonald, L., *To the Last Man, Spring 1918*, Viking. 1998.
6. Ibid.
7. Ibid.
8. Nobbs, H.G., *In Battle & Captivity 1916–1918*, Pen & Sword, 2014.
9. Marks, T.P.
10. Ibid.
11. *The Times History of the War Volume VI*, The Times, 1916.
12. Ibid.
13. Ibid.
14. MacDonald, L.
15. Ibid.
16. Middlebrook, M.
17. Middlebrook, M.
18. *The Times*.
19. van Emden, R., *Prisoners of the Kaiser*, 2000.
20. Hall, M., *In Enemy Hands*, 2002.
21. Ibid

Having made the decision to surrender, will the attacker accept it?

The moment of decision, to flee, fight on or surrender?

Captured French *poilus* (infantrymen) wait to be escorted to the rear. Apart from the photographer, no other Germans seem to be present; if they were, they would be with their prisoners.

Colonel Chantier, officer commanding the French 141 Infantry Regiment, is helped on his way to Germany by being provided with personal transport.

Belgian soldiers captured in Antwerp pose for a photo with their guards in Mechelen.

Many prisoners never left the immediate area behind the front. Here Russian prisoners are setting out to dig trenches.

An empty church was the ideal place for wounded and unwounded prisoners if there were insufficient men available to escort them to the railhead.

It was not always possible to get wounded prisoners to the rear so temporary aid posts were set up. This hut was taken over for use as a dressing station at the start of a Russian winter.

In the east losses were often very large. This column of Russians took nearly thirty minutes to pass the photographer.

As many Russians wanted to surrender anyway, what problem would a wounded Russian and two comrades be if left to make their own way back?

A soldier lying wounded was vulnerable. It might be easier for the captor to dispose of the wounded rather than waste time and resources on them.

A group of lucky French prisoners. They are being escorted for their lunch. Reading most accounts, such a scene was not the norm.

British captives, headed by their officer, are being marched through an area near Wervik, called America.

Russians taken prisoner near Lodz. After a battle, captured equipment was removed, often by the men who had just been using it.

Wounded French soldiers, after being treated, wait for orders to move to the rear.

A face that clearly shows what it is like to be a PoW.

A crashed and wounded British flyer being assisted by two German enlisted men, one of whom is wearing a British soldier's tunic.

When time permitted, officers questioned their prisoners to gain information about enemy dispositions and movements.

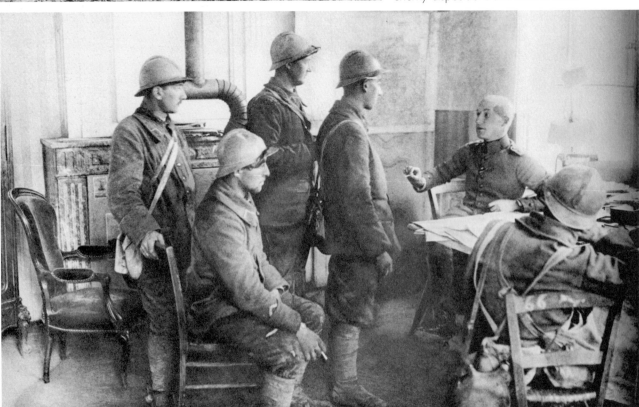

British prisoners and one armed guard behind locked gates somewhere in France.

British soldiers taken during the March Offensive, 1918, calmly wait to move to the rear. They are guarded by just one young, bored German. At times like these many would have been weighing up their chances of escape.

British troops with their escort marching through a French town on the Somme.

With no guards available to take them to the railhead, PoWs were kept in any any available space. At least they have been given a bucket to use as a toilet.

Prisoners were often seen as a trophy and photographed with their captors.

Photographed with their weapons, two of the three men ignore the camera while the third stares intensely at it. As they are still wearing their steel helmets they cannot be far back from the front.

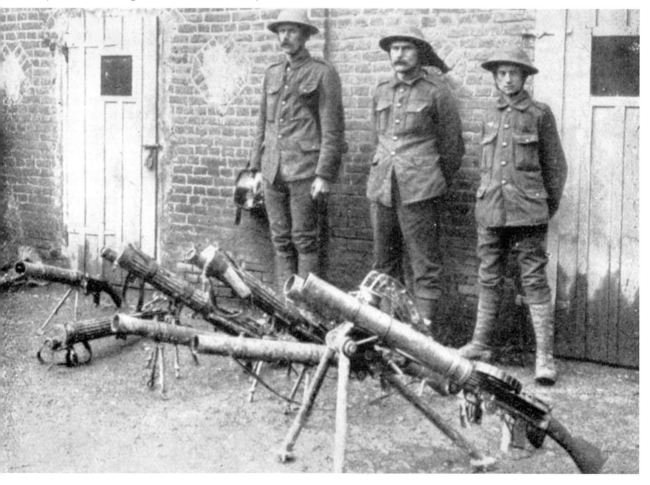

A surrendering officer was a prize. A crashed British pilot was a major prize and a must-see. As this flyer crashed well behind German lines he attracted a number of high ranking officers.

Sergeant Harrison was one of the lucky ones who quickly moved from missing to wounded and PoW.

Sergt. W. HARRISON, 2nd South Lancashire Regt., 55, Wilson Road, Reading.—Wounded and prisoner. He has been mentioned in dispatches and awarded the D.C.M.

Newly captured Russians being checked, for wounds and equipment, before being sent on to the rear.

With arms up signalling complete surrender, the potential prisoner was at his most vulnerable. Surrender en masse was usually a safer bet than alone.

Die Russen ergeben sich

A British soldier, badly wounded during the fighting near St Quentin, is being carried by his comrades. They are being taken to the rear by lightly wounded guards.

During the 1918 March Offensive there were so many captives that there were not enough men available to escort them. It was not uncommon after capture for prisoners to be told to make their own way to the rear, often through advancing Germans.

Some of the first Americans to be captured. Compare their size with that of their captors.

British troops captured in Belgium in the summer of 1917 await their fate. Again, just one man is guarding them.

Small groups of men were often taken to headquarters for interrogation. Here about twenty British soldiers are waiting their turn to meet an interrogator.

A large number of French soldiers waiting for their escort.

During the 1917 German attacks near Nieuport, many British prisoners were taken. Here they are being concentrated before the start of their journey to Germany.

Gruppe russischer Offiziere, welche sich zum Spaß mit deutschen Uniformen bekleiden, die sie den Gefangenen abgenommen haben

A group of newly captured Russian officers pose for their photo as if nothing has happened.

Chapter Two

Transportation to a New Life

Once captured, prisoners were moved, on foot, out of the combat zone as quickly as possible unless they were needed for work parties near the front. In the case of two officers' batmen, work was tasting captured food and drink in case it was poisoned. Quite pleasant as long as it wasn't, or unless you were teetotal as one of them was.

Some were immediately put to work helping move the German wounded to the rear and a few spent many months labouring immediately behind the fighting area often in appalling conditions suffering great privations. To make their life worse, British authorities did not know where they were so they received no Red Cross parcels and had to rely on their own skills to make sure they ate enough to stay alive.

The correct notification was essential. As a prisoner, you were missing and, after a while, presumed dead. This naturally would cause deep upset for family and friends, could have financial ramifications for those at home (unneeded mourning clothes, for one) and cause severe problems for the prisoner in the way of food and mail.

When no PoW notification was received, death was assumed. Captain Nobbs' family received the standard telegraph: 'Most deeply regret inform you Cap. H.G. Nobbs – London Regiment. Killed in Action Sept. 9.'[1] Prior to this, a letter to him from his family had been returned with a slip: 'Killed in action September 9'. The Army Council telegram was followed by one of sympathy from the King and Queen and then his name appeared in the official casualty list. To confirm that this was correct his family also received letters from the front that confirmed his death and also described the manner. He was not dead and this was not an isolated incident.

Some reservists called at the start of the war had prepared for the possibility of dying by taking out life insurance. As a result, Mrs Holland of Reading received a very special double Christmas present. Her husband Alfred had been recalled at the start of the war and been sent straight to the front. She received a telegram from the War Office informing her of her husband's death in action on 17 September followed by a letter of sympathy from Lord Kitchener. Her husband had taken out a life insurance policy in April with the London and Manchester Industrial Assurance Company. Upon receipt of the documents, they immediately paid his widow the sum she was entitled to – £25. A later telegram confirmed that he had been wounded and taken prisoner and was recovering in a camp in Germany. The company did not ask for a refund.

Receipt of the official telegram informing them their relative was a PoW, followed by a letter from them, allowed families to get on with their lives in reasonable confidence that they would see their son, husband, father again. PoW camp censorship was strict so the sender could only write a few bland words. A typical letter was sent by Private Walker of the Coldstream Guards to his mother. He was in Schneidemühl Camp. 'I am in the best of health and spirits under the circumstances. We are being fairly well treated by the Germans, though, of course, we feel it very much being parted from home and wives, and children. With longing wishes for peace.'[2] He had done his bit for the second time, having served in the South African War.

Private Easton of the RAMC stayed behind voluntarily to help the wounded. Early in the morning of the day after his capture he responded to calls from the Germans for volunteers to help the wounded British troops in the church. In the morning the German sergeant who had asked for volunteers thanked him for his help, saluted him and asked him to get the troops on the wagons when they arrived. Arriving at the railhead he supervised their loading and was then left standing. Eventually he was fed and then was given a strange request. He was asked to volunteer to remain and work near the front with the wounded. A hospital, 4 miles from the front, was being opened, so he consented to stay. For the sake of legality, he wrote in the German sergeant's diary that he voluntarily 'would proceed within 30 kilometres of the front with 625 Sanitäts Komp.'[3] He was even made an acting sergeant to give him authority over most of the German helpers.

The treatment of the newly-captured wounded varied considerably. It was about luck and being in the right place at the right time. Fusilier Hammond, wounded in the head, face, leg, hand and back, on 25 March 1918, had lost consciousness from his wounds. When he came round he saw a lone German walking up and down the road so he pretended to be dead. Eventually he decided to give himself up as it was getting dark. He could have been shot or bayoneted and no one would have been any the wiser but fortune smiled and the German was kind to him, making a crutch to help him move. Escorted to a Red Cross post he was given further good treatment and a proper dressing; Germany was suffering from cloth shortages so many bandages were made from paper.

Possibly because he was an officer or simply because he was lucky Captain Nobbs had a similar experience of German kindness. Lying badly wounded in a shell hole for two days he expected to die but then he heard a German call out to him. As he was blind from a bullet wound in the head he could not see the German and fearing the worst waited for a bullet or bayonet to finish him off. As he raised himself on one elbow the German put his arms round his body and helped him up but when he could not stand his captor placed both arms around him and dragged him to a trench. He eventually ended up in field dressing station.

Private Deane of the Durham Light Infantry recalled that on arrival at Limburg there was only a Russian orderly to deal with the wounded but there was a captured British doctor who was working on the worst cases. Fusilier Hammond found the treatment less than satisfactory when he arrived at a camp, and there were no proper bandages to be had. Captain Nobbs, although he was treated well, during the six days that had elapsed between him being found and his arrival in Hannover his wound had received no attention.

In major battles, prisoners, often regardless of their condition as long as they could walk, were sent off to the rear, often with the weakest of escorts; many thought of escape, some did, but most just marched. During the spring 1918 offensive, crossing what had been no man's land and the unoccupied German trenches was a very dangerous time, the reason being that whatever British artillery was still firing was bombarding the two, almost empty, areas.

Most prisoners started their march to a new life with just the clothing they were wearing when first taken, unless a German wanted it and a PoW had no way of stopping that happening. Lance Corporal Wortley, marching in a column to the rear on 21 March 1918, was stopped by a German who was much bigger than he was. He wanted Wortley's leather jerkin and 'simply took it'.[4] The Germans relieved them of everything else; sometimes they took their boots as well. Corporal Gale noted that 'you lost everything. Rifles naturally, but everything else as well. In my haversack I had tobacco and cigarette papers ... *that* went. All they left you was your gas mask. Then they started walking us back.' Lieutenant Crowder had a similar experience. Shortly after capture they took his 'British warm' (a short coat), field glasses and compass.

In volume 7 of *The Times History of the War*, published in 1916 it was noted that 'early in the war some of the German soldiers developed the habit of stripping both the dead and the wounded. As a typical example it told of Private Palin's experiences. His 'spine was pierced by a bullet in the battle of Mons. His legs became paralysed. The Germans stripped him of his clothes, and for two days and two nights he lay helpless on the field.'[5] Major Vandeleur, who escaped from Crefeld in December 1914, told that of his experiences after capture. He and other captives were placed in a large shed for the night with only a small amount of food, and that from the French Red Cross, and no straw. The only way they could keep warm was to walk all night because the Germans had taken their greatcoats.

This loss of possessions might happen immediately or behind the lines depending on whether the captors had time or not. On the first day of the German Spring Offensive, *Leutnant* Wedekind and his men approached a British position to find that 'they came out with their hands up – no weapons only steel helmets ... we had no time to look after them.'[6] Although the area was being bombarded, Wedekind noted that they 'just kept going back to our lines and I never saw them again.'[7]

It might have happened voluntarily, *Feldwebel* Gasser and *Gefreiter* Reinhard remembered. 'We followed up the creeping barrage quickly but, as soon as we appeared, the British threw away their weapons and surrendered. There really was no fight for Fayet. I think they were hoping for an opportunity to surrender. One of them gave me his razor. I think he wanted to thank me because he had been taken prisoner and not killed.'[8] Like many others, the German just waved him to the rear. Gasser found little opposition on 21 March. 'Small parties of enemy soldiers – from three to seven men – surrendered. They gave us cigarettes for which we gave them a friendly pat on the shoulder and sent them off to the rear.'[9]

Many British prisoners were their own jailors until they got further behind the front where they were collected together in holding stations. Jack Rogers' captor had merely asked for a cigarette, took a few when they were proffered, and then told him to dump his equipment and go.

In general, those taken prisoner were only briefly searched if they had been taken during an offensive – there was just no time for mobile troops to be thorough. Most pilfering would come later when they met rear echelon soldiers. For the attacking men it was the huge quantities of booty available that they were interested in, not a prisoner's belongings. There were far better things available.

During the Spring Offensive, smaller parties of prisoners gradually merged. As the columns increased in size they were given proper escorts. Prisoners of war made for good propaganda and improved morale at home. To this end many photographs were taken and used at home and in neutral countries to show German might. For those captured in small raids, after interrogation they would be sent straight back and put on a train for Germany. However during large scale battles the larger numbers of captives often meant that there were few buildings available for them and many would be herded into barbed-wire enclosures in fields with no protection from the elements and often no food or drink.

As they moved rearwards they were no longer guarded by the men from the battlefield but rear echelon soldiers whose bravery declined and poor behaviour increased the further back they went. Prisoners later recalled that they were never as considerate as the front-line German soldier. Indeed some were violent towards their new charges. Along the route, if they were fortunate, they received food from civilians as they passed through towns and villages. When they reached the railhead they were loaded on to the trains that would take them to their permanent prison camps in Germany. At this point there was probably a realisation that their life was no longer in any immediate danger but the presence of an armed guard would constantly remind them that they were no longer free men.

Most men arrived at their new home by train, usually slow and uncomfortable, with more thought being given to the horses than the men. A private in the Leicestershire Regiment told Captain Nobbs about his initial experiences. On the first night of captivity, not knowing what to do with their captives, the guards herded them together in a loose wire entanglement. They could only stand while it rained all night. They were then put in cattle trucks and sent into Germany with no food or water. On the second day, when they stopped, a lady came over to them with a can of soup which she poured on the rail in front of them.

On many occasions although food and drink were supplied to the guards, many British wounded were refused for long periods. In contravention to what the Red Cross stood for, in some cases the Sisters of the German branch of the organisation gave refreshment to the guards on the condition that they would not give it to the enemy soldiers.

Many English troops found that there was a national divide to the behaviour of the Germans. The French were reckoned to be treated far better than the British. Many signs displayed the words 'Gott Strafe England'. There was hatred for the British and contempt for the Russians. Among the English speaking nations, the Canadians were hated even more than the British and for some reason, for a time, preferential treatment was given to the Australians. The reason for favouring the French during Major Vandeleur's journey from the front was given in an official reply by the German government: 'If the English pretend that they were attended to during the journey only after the French, the reason is to be found in the quite comprehensible bitterness of feeling among the German troops, who respected the French on the whole as honourable and decent opponents, whereas the English mercenaries had, in their eyes, adopted a cunning method of warfare from the very beginning, and, when taken prisoners, bore themselves in an insolent and provocative mien.'

Private Gay, who was captured at Guillemont in July 1916, sheltering in a shell-hole hoping to make his way back, was taken prisoner and marched to the rear. He was put in a cattle truck with just a sawn-off tub in the middle for a toilet. On reaching Dortmund he was given a shower; the soap consisted of a splash on the head, and some potato water to drink.

While the men might have been transported by truck, officers went in relative comfort. Captain Evans went to his camp in Gütersloh in the comparative luxury of a second-class carriage, smoking cigars. The seriously wounded Captain Nobbs had a very different experience. He was dragged along trenches and stretchered to a dressing station, bounced in ambulances and put in the basement of a private house in use as a hospital. All he received to eat was one bowl of soup and a piece of bread and cheese after three days without food. He was then locked in a railway truck with two other badly wounded men and on arrival at St Quentin was taken into a hospital.

Eventually after a two-day train ride he arrived in Hannover where the wounded were left on the platform.

H.J. Clarke, a regular in the Suffolk Regiment, was captured in The Salient in May 1915. He recorded his journey to the camp near Giessen, in Hesse. 'We were taken charge of by Uhlans, settled down about 10.00pm at a place called Bacleate, occupied the church which they had made something like a pig-sty, distance about 12 miles from Ypres. Only too glad to get down that night … Our food consisted of dry bread and water, about 12.00 noon on Sunday 9th we were supplied with bread and raw bacon with coffee, left by tram for Courtrai, there boarded train, meeting with others who had been captured round about us. Occasional stops with also a brick or two every now and then at fellows who were looking out of the small space we were allowed for air … finally reaching our destination Giessen at 11.00pm on night of 10th. Passed a horrible night on the 9th, packed like sardines, sleeping under and over seats such as they were, our food on the 10th consisted of bread, butter and two sausages, which I am sorry to say someone was entitled to more than I was, thus losing my sausages, more coffee but as usual with no milk or sugar. On reaching our Camp we were once more issued with food (bread and water), on the whole we were getting well washed inside.'[10]

Initially the men had been met by crowds of Germans who were pleased to see so many men being taken. In 1914, a private in the Norfolk Regiment experienced such crowds. His were not spontaneous crowds, they were school children who had been specially brought to the railway station. Not content with looking at the prisoners they threw things at them.

Corporal Hall, 1st Life Guards, wounded and captured in October 1914, had a similar experience on the way to his camp. There were women, men and little children howling and in many cases spitting at the prisoners when the sentries made them get out of the train. While this was happening they stood by and laughed. Four years later, some of these same civilians would be behaving completely differently when the men left.

After the initial interest of columns of marching PoWs had dwindled, they became part of the street scene. No longer were they jeered or cheered, just watched as they marched. Captain Evans, RFC pilot, was surprised by his reception. Except on one occasion, for the whole of his journey to Germany the men on the train were not insulted or cursed.

What they did not realise on their arrival, was that their incarceration might be for many years and that those years of imprisonment would turn out to be a curious mixture: banality, mundaneness, harshness and frustration, discomfort, despair, intermixed at times with a few simple pleasures. Whatever happened, they would all emerge older, wiser and hardened to life's vicissitudes.

Notes

1. Nobbs, H.G.
2. *Reading Standard.*
3. van Emden, R.
4. Middlebrook, M.
5. *The Times.*
6. Middlebrook, M.
7. Ibid.
8. Ibid.
9. Ibid.
10. Hall, M.

French wounded being taken to the rear in August 1914. They had been taken prisoner by 26 Reserve Division during fighting near Schirmeck.

This group of French prisoners have brought the wounded with them. They are waiting patiently to enter the camp at Wimsdorf.

At the collection point, when enough guards were available, the men would march to entrain for transport to Germany.

Probably their last female contact for the next four years is sitting in the centre of the picture. These Englishmen were captured in 1914 and are waiting in the buffet at Lille station for their train to Germany.

A wounded officer would be provided with transport.

A large group of Serbian soldiers waiting their escort to the rear.

Three lucky British soldiers: they have been fed and given a hot drink.

Lucky French captives are being given drinking water; not something that happened for all prisoners.

Wounded British troops, captured near St Quentin, being carried or helped by their comrades. As they are wounded, the escort is very light.

French prisoners, taken on the Chemin des Dames, assist their captors by pulling German wounded to the rear.

A group of British soldiers on the Somme being guarded by a cavalryman, a medic and a foot soldier.

As well as being photographed for a keepsake, some prisoners were paraded and inspected by their enemy.

British and French officers under escort. The officer on the extreme left of the fore rank is Colonel W.E. Gordon, of the Gordon Highlanders.

On arrival at the railway station nearest to their new accommodation, the men were marched through the town to their destination. Initially a spectator sport, the civilians soon got bored with watching the marching columns. There is only one young girl watching this parade.

French North African troops, Saphis, wait to move to the train head.

Belgian troops with their escort.

A propaganda coup – vast numbers of prisoners being marched through Lille on their way to the station. The intention is clear: to show how powerful the German Army is.

French troops pushing wagons loaded with wounded compatriots.

French troops waiting in line to board their wagon. Only officers travelled in seated compartments.

Ankunft kriegsgefangener Franzosen

Begegnung gef. Franzosen u. deutscher Soldaten

German troops arriving at the railhead in horse wagons and French prisoners leaving in open-topped wagons; perhaps not too unpleasant in the summer but as they are wearing greatcoats it is probably cold.

Chapter Three

Camp Life and Death

Within the first six months of the war, more than 1.3 million prisoners were being held in camps across Europe. Modern research suggests that at least 7 million, and perhaps as many as 9 million, were taken prisoner during 1914–18. German prisoner of war camps alone held an estimated 2.4 million soldiers from thirteen nations by the end of the war; the biggest nationality among these captives were Russians, 1.4 million taken prisoner by October 1918, followed by more than 500,000 French prisoners. By 1915, as a result of battles such as the Masurian Lakes and Tannenberg, Germany already held over 1 million captives.

For both sides, PoWs often represented a considerable logistical problem. They had to be transported away from the battlefield, housed in secure conditions, sustained, and kept as stipulated under strictly defined conditions for the duration under mutually agreed conventions and agreements. Accommodating such a vast number of PoWs was a huge problem for all countries involved. And when war was declared, there was no system in place on either side for dealing with these unwanted guests.

There were four types of camp in Germany:

1. *Mannschaftslager* – Enlisted Men's Camp for soldiers and NCOs.
2. *Offizierslager* – Officer Camp for commissioned officers only.
3. *Internierungslager* – Internment Camp for civilians of enemy states.
4. *Lazarett* – military hospital for PoWs.

By the end of the war in the twenty-six Army Corps areas responsible for PoWs there were over 160 different camps, many with numerous sub-camps outside the main camp.

Camp type	Number of camps
Mannschaft	91
Offizier	51
Internierungs	5
Lazarett	20+

The following table indicates the size of the problem:

		10.8.1915	10.7.1916	10.6.1917	10.10.1918
Belgian	Officer	663	658	656	810
	O/rank	41,110	41,711	42,681	45,209
British Empire	Officer	656	890	1,911	4,456
	O/rank	24,730	27,634	45,863	177,553
French	Officer	4,499	5,973	6,908	10,865
	O/rank	264,890	348,832	388,897	524,546
Russian	Officer	6,081	9,288	9,920	14,050
	O/rank	702,613	1,225,154	1,244,815	1,420,479
Civilians interned		68,694	84,457	98,866	111,879
All countries total including civilians to end of year		1,408,066	1,804,660	1,909,131	2,526,922

By the end of the war the camps contained, according to German records, prisoners from thirteen countries. However, as any nationality that fought as part of the British Empire were recorded as English, it was considerably more. Some contingents were much larger than others for many different factors – puzzle for the reader.

Total number of prisoners
on 10.10.1918

Country	Officers	O/ranks
Russia	14,050	1,420,479
France	10,865	524,546
British Empire	4,456	177,553
Italy	4,589	128,331
Belgium	810	45,209
Romania	1,656	41,641
Serbia	4	27,908
Portugal	267	6,748
America	204	2,253
Japan	16	90
Greece	37	4
Montenegro	0	5
Brazil	0	2
Total	36,954	2,374,769

Unplanned for numbers meant that camps were often hastily set up according to need, utilising existing buildings: some were better than others, while many camps were built from scratch. The camp at Gütersloh was a converted sanatorium, Werl was in a monastery, Neisse, an officers' camp, was located in a former military academy in the centre of the town, Halle camp was a disused factory, Holzminden, a British officers' camp, was housed in a former cavalry barracks built in 1913. The camp at Danzig (Troyl) consisted of barges moored on the bank of the Vistula River, each containing 100–500 men. The administration block, kitchen and other facilities of the camp were on shore. Men from the failed Irish Brigade were sent to Troyl.

Some were small, others large. Most were for other ranks, some for officers, some were for specific branches of the forces or specific groups, or for purposes other than simple incarceration. The camp in the citadel at Mainz held just 700 men, while Soltau held 35,000 but had 50,000 registered working outside the camp. Limburg an der Lahn, holding 12,000 men, was a camp in which Irish prisoners were concentrated for the purpose of recruiting for the Irish Brigade, which few joined. Two Irishmen at the camp were shot, according to the Germans for attacking the sentries. British evidence showed it was because they were not prepared to become traitors and refused to join the Irish Brigade. Wahmbeck was a hotel holding mostly officers from the merchant service. Zossen, a camp 20 miles south of Berlin, was solely for British and French troops from India and Africa. They were subjected to propaganda urging them to revolt against their 'colonial masters'. Little success was recorded. All officers and men for internment in Switzerland were concentrated at Konstanz. There were two camps in Karlsruhe. The one in the grounds of the Karlsruher Schloss contained naval and, later, aviation officers, the other, the former Europäischer Hof, was known as 'The Listening Hotel', and was an interrogation centre.

By 1916 *The Times History of the War* was able to rank some of the camps. While there was little complaint about many, there was a range of camps which ran from good, even excellent, to terrible. In Mainz officers' camp, 'a spirit of contentment pervaded the entire prison';[1] Erfurt – good; Schloss Celle (civilian) – excellent; Burg – bad; Torgau and Wittenberg – terrible. In Wittenberg the men were looked upon and treated as criminals.

Wittenberg was complained about by the American Ambassador. He was concerned that it did not provide sufficient overcoats during the winter (sixteen overcoats between 278 British prisoners) and that a particularly vicious guard dog was brought into the barracks which attacked the prisoners and tore their clothes. 'Men were flogged with rubber whips, beaten at the whim of their guards and tied to posts with their arms above their heads for hours.'[2]

At Minden, a French priest reported that the German guards kicked British prisoners in the stomach, broke their guns over their backs and often starved them.

The wounded PoWs needed treatment. *Lazerett* 5 at Hannover was a typical camp set up to deal with them. After days of gruelling travel, the seriously wounded Captain Nobbs eventually arrived at the camp to be placed in Ward 43: nine beds, four British and four French officers. It was a converted military school where in the morning operations were performed on the prisoners and in the afternoon dealt with German military personnel suffering from STDs. Like many other camps, the regime was strict. No female nurse tended to them and there was no attempt to provide a diet that catered for the differing needs of the wounded. But according to Nobbs it was better than what was normally received in a standard camp. The downside was that he had to pay for it. He received an allowance from the German government who recovered the money from the British government who then charged it against his pay in England.

For those who recovered from severe wounds, repatriation was a potential life-line. Originally those unfit for further service were directly exchanged but later they were exchanged to live in camps in Switzerland. The severity of a man's wound did not guarantee release. Each had to be assessed and sometimes more than once depending on the whim of the doctor. Completely blind, Captain Nobbs would be unable to take up arms again, but still had to be examined. In Nobbs' case, 'the Examination Board consisted of a Swiss doctor, a German doctor, and the camp commandant. The Swiss doctor was provided with a schedule of disablements under which prisoners could be passed for exchange to their own country, and partial disablements for Switzerland.'[3] Frequent objections to a prisoner's application were made by the German representative. The decision was not final; there was a further medical examination at the border, this time only by German doctors. As a result some were returned to their camp. Those going to Switzerland were examined at Konstanz, those for Britain were examined at Aachen. Even though he had been passed for England Nobbs still had to wait a further two weeks before being sent home. On arrival in England he returned home and wrote his memoirs. He noted with irony that months earlier he had been deemed dead and his affairs had been put in order by his solicitors. One piece of mail was from the same solicitors asking for payment for 'services rendered in connection with'[4] his death.

Health was not the only reason for release. Article 9 of the 1906 Geneva Convention provides:

> The personnel charged exclusively with the removal, transportation, and treatment of the sick and wounded, as well as with the administration of sanitary formations and establishments … shall be respected and protected under all circumstances. If they fall into the hands of the enemy they shall not be considered as prisoners of war.

Captain C.T. Edmunds, RAMC, who had been captured at the start of the war, was a prisoner in Magdeburg Camp. On 12 January, his family received a pleasant surprise:

their son arrived home without notice. He was one of five British Army doctors who had been released on 10 January. There were more, so the question of who should have been released had been 'settled by drawing of lots by matches'.[5]

Early camps were quickly overcrowded, but this situation improved once makeshift camps were replaced. In Germany many of the PoWs were employed to build their own camps. By the end of the war there were 200 parent camps in 21 autonomous Army Corps districts. Each camp was also autonomous and most had smaller camps attached which supplied men for *arbeit Kommandos* so that nearly 1 million prisoners were working in Germany in industry or agriculture by the end of 1916.

Conditions varied between camps and in the same camp over the duration of the war. A major factor was the commandant: some were benign, some malevolent, some hated the English. Private Rogers of the Sherwood Foresters at Münsterlager found that his commandant fell into the latter category and took every chance to let the prisoners know it. The Russians had a reputation for being the dirtiest people in the camp, using a corner of their barracks as a latrine, while the British were reputedly the cleanest. Whenever the commandant felt like it he made everyone move barracks. The British were always allocated to the Russian barracks and the Russians to the British. One rainy Sunday, their day off, the British were marched around the camp until the commandant was bored. The British were always addressed as 'Schweinhunde'.

At one camp the commandant allowed his guards to train the dogs to bite English soldiers. Boys with bows and arrows were allowed in one camp where they could shoot at the prisoners with arrows tipped with nails. In Süd-Edewechter Moor camp, to discourage his men from being too friendly, the commandant offered a prize to the first guard to shoot a prisoner who went into the prohibited zone between the wires surrounding the camp.

Not all Germans behaved badly to the prisoners but those who got caught being nice could be punished. In early 1917 'a number of inhabitants of a North German town had been found guilty and sentenced to varying terms of imprisonment for improper and unpatriotic conduct towards prisoners of war and that their names had been published and themselves exposed to shame that their falsity might be made known to generations of Germans to come.'[6] Their crime was to have taken pity on some Canadian prisoners in transit through the town and provided them with food and drink.

Some hated the British, others didn't, but as commandants could be replaced, a good camp could change quickly, as did Wittenberg: 'the camp of horrors'.[7] A new commandant and better methods improved the camp.

It is easy to choose just three categories of camp but inside these there were differing levels: good, bad and awful, with the definition varying as to whether it was an officer or other-ranks camp.

Wittenberg was a particularly unpleasant camp. As a result of the poor barrack arrangements a typhus epidemic broke out in December 1914. The German authorities immediately cordoned off the camp and left. Any communication was by shouting through the wire entanglements and food and other supplies were pushed over by means of chutes.

In February 1915, six British medical officers, three of whom died while in the camp, were sent to look after the situation. The harrowing report compiled by the surviving officers was a scathing indictment of the lack of care and the level of inhumanity.

They found 'an appalling condition of things, many ill, many without attention, dirt, neglect and semi-starvation everywhere. In the improvised hospital there were no mattresses. Sick prisoners were hidden everywhere in the camp, refusing to go into the hospital. There were no stretchers to carry the typhus cases on. They had to be carried on tables from which men ate. As these tables could not be washed, they proved an effective means of conveying the disease.'[8] The Germans 'refused to permit the most elementary precautions to be taken.'[9] Their food was insufficient: half a *petit pain*, half a cup of milk and soup, carried in a wooden tub that had no cover, that contained dirt and dust. Delirious men waved their arms, brown to the elbow with faecal matter. Patients were crammed together on the floor so tightly it was difficult to walk between them. They were lice-ridden. Few drugs and bandages were available. 'Bed sores were common ... toes or the whole foot were attacked by gangrene, dressings were not available to treat them, and consequently the limbs had to be amputated.'[10] Dr Aschenbach, the German camp doctor, visited only once. 'He came attired in a complete suit of protective clothing, including a mask. He made a brief and rapid inspection and did not return.'

Gardelegen camp, between Berlin and Hannover, was as bad as Wittenberg and it too was troubled with typhus in 1915. Epidemics of examathous typhus also broke out at Stendal, Langensalza, Schneidemühl and at Cassel-Niedzwehren. Camps might contain men from any or all of the Allied countries; segregated, this was not a problem, but in camps where they were completely mixed so they could 'learn to know one another',[11] as at those mentioned above, there were health risks. Many Russians carried typhus and mixing them in with other nationalities caused it to spread quickly.

Mixing up the different nationalities, as few could speak a different language, made communication difficult, probably what the guards wanted. As a result, in other ranks' camps an ersatz language developed based around English, French, German and Russian. '*Veil camarades for Kommando, tavarish, veil Franzosen, veil Rusky veil arbeit. You nix?*' This translates into 'I hear there are a big lot of French and Russians down for Kommando, Rusky: are you for it?' This was not a problem in an officers' camp were a second language was not uncommon.

Inadequate food (for which the Allied naval blockade was partly responsible), poor housing, bad sanitation, the nature of some of the work assigned to prisoners and the brutal behaviour of the guards were the constant complaints about German camps. Life for PoWs in Turkish camps, except for officers, was especially harsh.

The living conditions of the men were a cause of complaint, but there was little that prisoners could do about it. Insufficient fuel and not enough blankets meant almost constant cold; insufficient ventilation at night fouled the atmosphere spreading contagion quickly; there was no privacy; men slept in bunks or beds of wood or wood and netting – it was far from comfortable.

Guards, like their commanders, came in a variety of guises. Some were helpful and friendly, some just did their jobs dispassionately, others openly displayed their hatred. The majority were unfit for any other form of service and some had issues because of that. Private Stevens of the Middlesex Regiment had the full range of guards, the young dregs who could not serve at the front and the elderly who were short tempered. One they called 'Drippy because his nose always ran'[12] was thought to be in his seventies and was very nasty. 'He'd swear at anybody and was not a man you could reason with in any way.'[13]

In an attempt to protect the prisoners, inspectors from neutral countries were called upon to check and report on camp conditions. But they were not given unrestricted access so many things went unseen. While they were able to report their findings it did not mean that anything would change and often the men were used as pawns in a game between the two countries for political reasons.

How much truth there might be in some of the reports is explained by the observations of a Leicestershire Regiment private. Technically prisoners were able to complain to the visiting inspector but this was not always possible and could require considerable strength of character. Before the inspection the commandant put up a notice that they had no reason to complain to the inspector and that if they did the punishment was fourteen days' imprisonment. As they stood there on parade, accompanied by the commandant and another German officer, he asked if there were any complaints. Two men were brave enough to complain. Two men received fourteen days.

Many PoWs were made to work. This was not so with officers who had a higher status and could only be asked to supervise the work of their men. Officially this work could be no closer than 30 kilometres to the front, but with manpower always short, many newly captured men were put to work at the front. All work was to be non-military but this was stretched near the front to include carrying ammunition and basically any job that needed doing. Official complaints brought either denial or retaliation. Once away from the front, the type of work given depended on local circumstances. Men with trades were fortunate in that there was a shortage of skilled labour in Germany and they were valued. They often replaced men at the front and worked away from the camp or sometimes in the camp where there was a need for their skills. Work was done for a derisory payment, and only then if prisoners were lucky. A token amount was given to them in worthless 'camp coupons' rather than real currency, so it did not greatly improve their lot in camp.

Without parcels from home provided by family and friends and/or the Red Cross, prisoners survived on a meagre ration of black bread and watery soup. Food, particularly the bread, was so precious that men constructed their own small scales to weigh each piece, and crumbs were carefully collected. This bread, usually given out at teatime for the next day, rarely lasted until bedtime: hunger was too pressing. Rifleman Humphreys, of the Post Office Rifles, used to take his and boil it in acorn coffee to make an unpalatable but slightly more filling meal. The next morning most would go to work hungry. Eventually, along with their parcels, each man would receive a bread ration, sent from Switzerland but paid for in Britain. One reason for the lack of parcels was the cost. The Hull PoW Fund asked for people to volunteer to look after a prisoner. There were over 350 prisoners to help but only 157 people volunteered to provide, at a monthly cost of £2, three 10lb parcels of food and 13lbs of bread. It was a lot of money.

Dr Ohnesorg, Assistant American Naval Attaché in Berlin, reported what he found during a visit to Giessen in December 1915, where 1,375 men lived in the camp and 601 were attached but worked out of the camp. His report was sent to the American Ambassador in London and then to the British Foreign Office. He reported that 'there is a great deal of friction between the German authorities and the British Prisoners of War over the question of work and numerous complaints were made regarding the treatment which men received at working camps. At least two gave details of being struck by a German soldier or civilian. They are employed in agricultural work, various industries, foundries and rolling mills, mines, quarries, etc.'[14]

Captain Nobbs, recovering in Hannover *Lazarett* camp, heard from a private in the Royal West Kents captured at Mons, about how the Germans used fear to try to make men do illegal work. When seventy British PoWs found that their intended work was making munitions they all refused. Even when threatened by their guards they still refused. 'Then they were taken out and made to stand in a row against a wall; and a firing-party was drawn up in front of them with loaded rifles, but not one of them flinched.'[15] Told they would be shot they all still refused. Fortunately the threat was not carried out and they were sent back to camp. On another occasion, men refused to work in a salt mine. They were threatened and when this had no effect, a man was taken away and a shot heard. Another man was taken and another shot heard. The men continued to refuse the work. Again it was a fake and the men were sent back to camp. A private in the Norfolk Regiment recalled that these men were sentenced to between twelve and fifteen months' imprisonment and that as a result of the poor treatment in prison one became insane.

Not everyone was as strong willed or principled, especially when the Germans stopped their food parcels. Towards the end of 1916, at Krupp's alone there were in excess of 1,500 Frenchmen working, alongside many other nationalities.

Rifleman Hall had arguments about how long and how often he should work, culminating in flaming rows about Sunday working. Private J. Land and the 'farmer and engineer rowed. Land struck both men, the engineer took up a hammer at Jimmy (just like this infernal squareheaded 84 round the waist nation) [sic.].'[16] Land 'narrowly escaped court-martial.'[17] Hall also records four men shot for refusing to work in a munitions factory and others bayoneted and bruised for minor offences. Later in the year he recorded that Logan of the King's Own had been bayoneted to death for a paltry offence.

There were many different ways to die. Some died naturally, through disease, although some of these deaths could have been prevented with better conditions or treatment. Some died of the wounds they had received, which with better treatment they might have survived. Others died of accidents, some of neglect, some of suicide, and then there were manslaughter and murder victims. In this latter category, differences between the German and British Army were clearly shown. The British Army brooked no form of physical assault by an officer or NCO on an enlisted man; however in the German Army such a rebuke was tolerated and indeed normal. With each camp being run independently, the level of control varied. How many men died as a result of violence will never be known but it was certainly not an insignificant number.

In the camps men were punished, often with violence, a rifle butt in the back or legs was common, to make them obedient. The same occurred outside the camp but without the control of the camp, the level of violence often increased with distance from that control. Away from the camp there were no real restrictions. There were many complaints about treatment at work or on the journey. In the mines if production was insufficient men would get hit with a shovel to spur them on. RAMC Private Easton told how 'guards could be brutal … one or two would take it out on you if they got you on your own. Some would hit you just as a matter of habit, on a march if you struggled a bit, they'd go along hitting you into position. Others, if they thought you were dodging work, would give you a clout.'[18]

Although conditions had improved at Wittenberg it was still a harsh, strictly disciplined camp. If a man refused to work, the commandant in 1916 issued an order that allowed the guards to use their weapons as needed. He enjoined the guards energetically to 'keep the prisoners at work. Should the attitude of the prisoner demand the use of weapons, this should be employed without regard to consequences. In the first place, the bayonet only is to be employed.'[19]

Reprisals against PoWs resulted in mistreatment and sometimes death. In 1916 when the French sent German prisoners to North Africa, and also when the British used Germans as workers for the BEF, the Germans sent newly captured French and

British prisoners to the Eastern front in reprisal. There they carried out forced labour in extreme conditions with little food; many died of starvation and exposure. Captain Nobbs noted that while he was a PoW, 200 men from Döberitz camp were sent to work in Poland as a reprisal for the British using Germans near the front line. Further reprisals occurred in 1917 when Germany had British and French prisoners of war carrying out forced labour in dangerous locations on the Western Front. This was as a result of the British and French using forced German labour on the Western Front but more because German prisoners had been forced to work for months under shellfire on the Verdun battlefield.

There was no sanctity in death for some. The norm was that when a man died he was buried, however primitively. Bill Easton saw that in the hospital at Condé, the dead were sometimes given post-mortems by trainee doctors who would cut them up but not sew them up again. Using paper bandages and adhesive, those PoWs on punishment were sent down to put them back together. Sometimes the students would cut the cadaver to pieces making the work very difficult.

The dead sometimes received other forms of abuse. During the typhus epidemic in Wittenberg, 'So many died that there was not room for all, and the coffins were piled one above another.' 'What the prisoners found hardest to bear … were the jeers with which the coffins were frequently greeted by the inhabitants of Wittenberg who stood outside and were permitted to insult their dead.'[20]

For many there was no love lost between the two nations. Rifleman Hall's sentiments were probably reciprocated by his employers: he had 'never met a filthier illmannered (sic.) race of people than the Germans'.[21] Hall, like many others, developed a hatred for the Germans and wanted to 'wipe a few items off a full slate'[22] when the war finished. Captain Nobbs recorded similar thoughts from one soldier he spoke to. 'If we ever see a German in England when we get back we will kill him'[23] and from another, 'when the war is over any German who is met in England by any prisoners of war will have a rough passage. There won't be any need to hold ourselves back any longer. My goodness, sir, they'll never get away alive!'[24] Unfortunately few Germans were prosecuted and any punishment received was minor.

The camps varied in size but most housed hundreds and sometimes thousands all in closely packed huts surrounded by watch towers and barbed wire. While some where built near industrial plants to discourage bombing, many were there purely to provide the needed labour. Some camps were better than others and the work they were detailed for varied: those providing work in agriculture were better than those who serviced a salt mine. If you were lucky like Private Spriggs of the MGC, taken at Cambrai in 1917, there was little work done. For the two months he was at Dülmen he just sat around. However Rifleman Ernest Evanson, captured on 1 July 1916 and sent to the same camp, spent twelve hours a day felling trees.

Although those employed in agriculture were generally better off than many other PoW workers, it was not always easy, especially for town-dwellers. Digging potatoes from 6.45am to 7.00pm with only a forty-minute break for a meal was back-breaking work. 'At Altdam prisoners were harnessed to the farming machinery, six men to a harrow and twelve to a plough, thus replacing one and two horses.'[25] Without parcels to look forward to, spending the day working in the fields, in freezing conditions, would have broken many.

Not everyone made it to an official camp. Some were kept near the front while others like Spriggs were moved back towards the fighting area. Some moved from one camp to another as dictated by circumstances. Captain Evans, after three weeks at what he thought was his new home, Gütersloh, was sent, along with all the flying officers who had been captured on the Somme, to Clausthal. As an officer, the authorities would have been notified. It was not that simple for other ranks, such information might never be sent or would be processed very slowly.

Some suddenly found themselves moved from being in an *Arbeit Kommando* to being in a *Strafe Kommando* (or punishment unit) for a petty reason or for no reason at all that they were aware of. Some could get caught in a vicious circle, where surviving one *Kommando* meant movement to another. This happened to Rifleman Hall who survived an ironworks only to be sent an iron mine, all the time with no parcels or communication. The issue of communication was paramount to the prisoners for family and nutritional reasons.

Although forbidden by the Geneva Conventions, many did work that helped the German war effort. Most did it without thought; those that did think about it probably worked out that it was easier to do as they were told in order to escape a clout or worse. Orders were orders and the penalty for disobedience could be fatal. In late 1918, a Hull soldier was smoking at roll call: forbidden and punishable. His punishment was such a severe beating from the guard that he died. The guard was not punished at the time or after the war.

Punishment and brutality were constants in the life of a PoW. At Sennelager a number of North Sea fishermen had their beards, moustaches and hair shaved off. A common punishment, often for very minor offences, was being tied to a post, sometimes in the snow. Being tied to a stake for a number of hours was as common as was sack drill: running around, with a 30lb sack your back, four times consecutively for fifteen minutes with a two-minute rest between. Some were punished with solitary confinement, while in some camps they were held over barrels and beaten with sticks. Men were slashed with swords, had their ribs broken by rifle butts, were forced to work in peat bogs in water up to their knees with only a blanket as clothing, on meagre rations, made to stand nearly naked in the rain, placed in dark cells with virtually no food, sentenced to servitude in a military prison (a total of 760 men) or bayoneted to death. Released prisoners told of further tortures: 'A man would be stripped and put in a bath. A German NCO would rub him hard with a very hard brush and sand, hitting him with the brush until skin was rubbed away and blood drawn.'[26] Two French brothers who escaped in mid-1917 told of a particularly lethal torture they had seen. The Turkish bath 'was mainly applied to men who refused to do munitions work ... the man would be shut in a very hot room until at the point of fainting. Then he would be dragged out and thrown, with little or nothing on, into the open air, sometimes into the snow. This would be repeated at intervals for some weeks. When they were returned to camp many died shortly afterwards from galloping consumption.'[27] Prisoners at Sennelager were punished by the 'roof'. The offender was hoisted on a tarred roof and exposed there for hours. Such treatments did not just happen to the British. Each nationality suffered and in many camps it was the Russians who fared the worst.

Whether in an official or unofficial camp, everyone had one problem in common, unless they were officers who generally received better rations and had far more parcels sent to them: that problem was food. Rifleman Evanson recorded 'how potato peelings came to be regarded as a luxury and how glad he was of the occasional chance of dipping his hands into the swine tubs'.[28] They should, according to international agreements, have been receiving foodstuffs roughly equivalent to that provided to a frontline German soldier. With lack of labour, shortages and the Allied blockade, this did not happen, and the PoW was always hungry and food always on their minds.

Constant hunger led to petty theft; food pilfering from the Germans (who were fair game), and from each other, which soured relationships. Agricultural working parties could secrete food such as a small potato to eat later, but if caught they would be punished. Working in the cookhouse gave them greater access to food but this was restricted to a lucky few. Some could barter what little they had – for example a wristwatch for a slice of bread with a German guard – but most soon ran out of things to barter until the parcels arrived.

While ironworks and mining were the worst jobs to be detailed for, probably the best job a prisoner could land was working in the camp cookhouse where the daily food was prepared in large vats. It was then placed in whatever containers were available and distributed to each man. The individual then had the choice to eat or save whatever was in their mess-tin. Few could resist the solution to their pain and consumed it immediately.

Like Spriggs, Evanson was suddenly moved, but for the better. He spent the happiest six months of his captivity in Minden *Lager*. 'Parcels from home came regularly. There was a British Army chaplain, a library, a school where men of the London regiment taught French, German, maths and music, a band and a male voice choir of fifty voices (their favourite rendering, *Excelsior*).'[29] The camp commandant was the nicest German he ever met and he obtained a cushy job in the camp office. Then in

March 1917 he found himself at Westerholt Camp in the Ruhr. From being an office worker he was suddenly a coal miner.

Private Clarke of the Suffolks was surprised to find that his new barracks at Giessen were 'not at all bad, in fact much better than anyone ever dreamed of'.[30] However, like Evanson, food was an issue. 'Horrible time until parcels arrived, in all about five weeks, fellows looking terribly bad.'[31]

Day in, day out, food 'meant little more than starvation rations. Typically, each man would receive a mug of ersatz coffee made from burnt barley or acorns, and a thin slice of black bread' mixed with potato and often sawdust. Lunch time soup was often just the water the guards had boiled their food in, with perhaps some vegetable pieces floating around. Those working behind the lines often received no meal and resorted to eating grass and collecting kale and nettle leaves to boil up later. If they were lucky they may have been able to add potato peelings.

The parcels did not always arrive when they should have done. Rifleman Hall's diary of 19 February 1916 recorded the arrival of his mother's Christmas parcel the day before and that it was not in the best of condition. However, his birthday parcel did arrive in goodish condition. The usual reason the authorities gave for a parcel being delayed was that it had been poorly packaged and not the result of petty larceny. While working on a farm where he was being fed and in very good health, Hall wondered in his diary what PoWs would look like without their parcels from home. Each parcel had to be taken to the censor's room for examination before they could be taken away and the contents enjoyed.

It was not just food that they needed, as underage soldier William Dunn of 1 Battalion Royal Berkshire Regiment told his family at home in a letter published in the local paper. Imprisoned in Meinster Camp, he wrote home that he was 'well but food is scarce, and warm clothes welcome, as the weather is very cold'.[32] He was thankful for the parcels received, the paper stated, adding that he was only sixteen years and eight months old and that he was an only son.

The Allied blockade caused shortages of raw materials in Germany and at the bottom of the pile for receiving materials were the PoWs. Dr Ohnesorg reported that in late 1915 British PoWs in Giessen did not have adequate clothing. Although it was winter 'a very large majority were without greatcoats, a great number were without suitable shoes and many without underclothing and socks. They stated that their names had been noted several times in regard to clothes needed but that nothing had come of it, and that in general it was impossible to obtain clothes upon application to the German authorities.'[33] While the majority were in uniform, many were in part dressed in French uniform and others in civilian clothing, but all was shabby. In 1916 Hall noted in his diary that boots were letting in the water and wondered how to overcome this problem – there were no spare boots or leather to repair what they had. To make the prisoners stand out if they did escape, and to stop their clothing from being mistaken for sporting attire, their uniforms had been decorated with a red strip along the outer surface of the arms and a broad one down the middle of the back.

Dental problems were common and a man could expect little comfort if his teeth were extracted. Rifleman Hall's entry in his diary for 16 October 1916 noted that he and a friend had teeth out and that on the 27th of the same month he had two more out, an experience, he recorded, that he was unlikely to forget.

Some of the PoWs required medical help for their wounds and although doctors were bound by the Hippocratic Oath, a patient's care was not always to the standard that was needed. 'Moreton of the 12th London Regt. died in hospital at Giessen. He was seriously wounded at Ypres on 8/5/15 and at Giessen his left leg was amputated at the thigh, but the job was bodged for after a while the bone protruded through the skin and another piece of bone was taken off. This was again unsuccessful and again a like operation was performed. Before he was thoroughly well again he was taken for a hot bath, placed in a bath and forgotten about for one and a half hours. He contacted cramp in the bath, and was unable to move. The water, of course, got cold and – he died. KULTURED COUNTRY THIS.'[34]

Fusilier Hammond of the Lancashire Fusiliers found the treatment lacking as well. Wounded by a bullet through his head and punctured by shrapnel, the camp he was sent to had no German doctors only Russian. Apart from the previously noted paper bandages (actually woven paper fibres like crêpe paper) there was little or no proper treatment available. He was just bandaged up and left. Only when his hand swelled up was treatment provided: a Russian doctor lanced it, saving his hand.

Iseghem hospital, although the English prisoners told the American representative of their own accord that they were happy with their treatment and care, was not a pleasant place to be sent. The *Daily Mail* reported just how unpleasant it was: 'This hospital was in the charge of a very clever, but very brutal doctor. My mate and I … were placed in beds opposite the operating room and saw far more of what was going on than we liked. The doctor did not believe in using chloroform. He used it as seldom as ever he could, particularly on Englishmen. He would do all kinds of operations without it. He would take a mallet and a chisel and get a bit of bone off a man's leg with the man in full senses.'[35] This was confirmed by Canadian soldier Private McPhail who had been wounded near Ypres. When he arrived at Iseghem hospital he was blind in one eye, when he left he was blind in both. Held down by three attendants and a sister, and without chloroform, he had his eye cut out. The cut was too deep and destroyed the nerve of the other eye.

A hospital in Hannover performed operations without anaesthetic. At Mülheim, dangerously wounded men were made to take baths in the open in bitter weather. 'Bandages were left on until they reeked.'[36] The wounded were often treated brutally.

This was not always the case, as Walter Humphreys of the Post Office Rifles found. He badly damaged his knee while, illegally, laying electric cable over the barbed wire of the Hindenburg Line before the German withdrawal to the position. It became so bad that the personnel at the work camp could not deal with it and took him to a German field hospital. After a successful operation he was kept in for weeks to recover. He felt he was well treated while he was there because he had received the same rations as the German wounded on the ward.

Whether or not it was true, British PoWs felt that the Germans treated the French better. Rifleman Hall, a town-dweller, was sent to work on the land. His work party moved out of the camp and were given the village gymnasium as their barracks. A party of Frenchmen were also detailed for the same work but they were billeted in the village inn. Perhaps a random choice but the British did not think so. Contradicting this, he later wrote in his diary of the arrival of 260 Frenchmen who had been working behind German lines: 'May I never behold again such specimens of humanity. With hollow eyes and sunken cheeks, their clothes hanging on them like sacks, torn and filthy, starved into semi-insanity, they rushed the guards, broke through the barbed wire and ran to us for food. That which we gave them, although as hard as iron, disappeared rapidly. It was of course impossible to feed all, the late comers ran to the waste tubs and scrambled for refuse.'[37]

There were sometimes theatrical entertainments to take men's minds off their situation. Camps usually had a theatre, not necessarily designated as such but a building large enough to accommodate an audience. Using what materials were available they managed to construct a stage of some description. Chairs had to be brought in for the performance. The shortage of women was quickly overcome with the judicious use of padding and whatever could be made or scrounged to transform a male into a female. Improvisation was the key. Most concerts comprised singing and comedy but some troupes performed known plays and sometimes plays written by themselves. Naturally the best seats in the house would go the Germans. Without the presence of the Germans the same sorts of entertainment occurred spontaneously in the barracks.

Concerts were not only theatrical. There were often many talented musicians in a camp and once instruments had been borrowed, bought locally or received from home, bands and orchestras were formed. Much of the success and quality of performances by actors and musicians depended on how benevolent the camp commandant was. Some went to great lengths to assist, others did not. As well as taking men's minds off the war, they also temporarily forgot their hunger.

Camp inmates ran education classes and produced newspapers and magazines – there were often journalists, academics and cartoonists who could share their skills, and libraries were run with books sent from Britain. Most news was brought into the camp by new arrivals. Although the Germans provided official bulletins and an English language paper, *Continental News*, daily, few believed what was written. According to Nobbs it contained 'lies of the worst description'.[38]

Then there was sport and athletics to occupy the mind. All these myriad aspects of life might be captured on camera and sent home, courtesy of inmate amateur photographers or more usually a German civilian. Tens of thousands of cards were sent home to show that things were alright – great propaganda for the Germans because the cards were censored so people in Britain only saw what they were intended to see – an unreal version of camp life which was reinforced by the letters sent home by prisoners.

The weather directly impacted on life in and out of camp. Spring and summer sun made life more bearable. For those stationed out of the camps the snow also could help improve their life, if only for a short while. During the winter of early 1917, although it was not permitted, Rifleman Hall and his friends at Mensfelden, near Giessen, 'begged and stole sledges and tobogganed to'[39] their hearts content.

A life in agriculture was to be preferred to the life of a *Strafe Kommando*, cut off from others and, importantly, from their parcels. Hall went from farm work to an ironworks for striking a fellow prisoner. The prison cells were designed to be unpleasant but he recorded that the ironworks was Hell. He worked from 4.30am to 9.30pm on his work day and noted in his diary that 'the food is putrid. Treatment unhuman and terribly hard work being driven like niggers (*sic*.) from morning till night.'[40] Living on swede and mangel-wurzel soup, ersatz black coffee with no sugar and a round of bread a day quickly meant starvation. But there was always the hope of return to the main camp or better still prisoner exchange.

Starvation reduced many to skin and bone, their flesh hanging loose. It slowed movement and made men think only of themselves – no one else mattered; their survival became paramount. Starvation meant death for some and each camp had its own cemetery to testify to the hardships of prison life: many deaths were through starvation or through a disease like typhus which they were too feeble to fight. Norman Cowen recalled how potatoes actually killed some of the men in his camp, rather than help save them. When typhus spread in his camp, many died of the infection. For some reason the Germans suddenly provided a sack of potatoes which they put in the ashes of the stove and pulled them out half raw. 'Their stomachs could not manage that and so it sort of distended them and killed them.'[41]

One man's death could improve the chances of another man surviving. When the parcels arrived, any for those deceased would go into a pool and the food handed out. For many they were indeed lifesaving.

By 1916 the processing of parcels from the many organisations formed to help prisoners was rationalised and centralised under the International Red Cross. Parcels provided food, clothing and many others things a prisoner needed, like soap, a very useful product to barter with as Germany could not produce enough. The parcels were as useful to the Germans as they were to the British. Their slow release could help control the prisoners, it meant they did not have to provide as much food to them at a time of great civilian food shortages and, with theft and bartering, it helped feed some of them.

In better camps parcels were dealt with by the British under the watchful eyes of German supervisors. With a 13lb food parcel, containing essentials like tea, cigarettes, biscuits, cheese, tinned milk and dripping, arriving every fortnight, some were able to stop eating German food and give it to the Russians who received no help, or trade it for jobs. Each prisoner also received a fresh bread ration, cooked in a neutral country and shipped to them. During the summer when the bread would go off they received hard biscuits instead.

Captain Nobbs, who because of his injuries spent some time mixing with other ranks, noted that the Russians 'seemed to be the least provided for, and parcels for them were very rare. They lived or rather starved on the German rations: and when men have to work or remain in the open air all day such a ration was a form of torture.'[42] With their parcels the British were not always dependent on the rations and in return for a Russian carrying the soup dixie, they would give him a cup of the watery liquid potato. 'So hungry were the Russians … that hundreds of them would wait hours in the cold on the off-chance of a few getting the job.'[43]

There could be a downside to suddenly receiving better quality food. Many of those who did, unused to solid foods, suffered from boils.

The parcel system worked well, but if the recipient moved camp it could be weeks before the parcel caught up with the prisoner. For the inmates of less benevolent camps the arrival of parcels would go unnoticed as they were put in storage and released only after thorough inspection to check for escape materials. Indeed, some would never see their parcel because of its theft by a guard who could not bear to see his enemy eating like a lord while his family was starving.

Officers received more parcels but had to pay the Germans for their food. Newly arrived officers might not be able to pay for their food, but usually other officers would assist them until they could pay for it themselves. When the charge for officers' food was reduced by international agreement, it was a good excuse to reduce the quality and quantity of the food provided. Naturally, for extra payment the original level could be continued.

Receiving mail from home was almost as important as parcels to a prisoner's sense of well-being. Mail allowance for officers was of course more generous. They could receive as many as they were sent and of whatever length and with less stringent censorship. Outward mail was restricted though: two letters of four pages each, and four postcards a month. Letters were censored in the camp and held for a number of days before being released.

As a result of their incarceration many officers and men developed a psychological condition termed 'barbed-wire disease': an irrational feeling of claustrophobia. PoW camps were zoo-like with German civilians coming to view the inmates. Some lost heart from the time the camp doors closed; 'their spirits gradually sank, their bodies with them until to live became too great a burden. They just passed away.'[44] 'A lot of men ... died just of worry and anxiety,'[45] remembered ex-PoW Bill Easton. But most did not die, even though they felt like not continuing with their boring, starving lives. Sometimes it affected groups of men: 'It was a common sight in the camp to see a group sitting around not saying a word or muttering a sound – just sitting there, brooding silently.'[46] Some went mad and were taken to the asylum, others committed suicide.

Officers had different problems in camp. They 'led a life of almost pampered ease. Their grouses centred on such things as the quality of the wine, the availability of tennis courts and the shortcomings of the orderlies who waited on them. But being treated as gentlemen of enforced leisure rather than as slave labourers – all play and no work – had its drawbacks. Boredom was the big problem. And life behind barbed wire for this privileged class could be just as much a test of character and mental stamina as in the working camps of the downtrodden Tommy.'[47]

Captain Nobbs, at Osnabrück, described his living quarters as 'comfortable',[48] a small stove with coal was provided, and the furniture consisted of 'camp-beds with two blankets each, a chest of drawers and a small table and chair.'[49] No rooms were overcrowded. Accommodation for officers was always better, even when they were being punished for trying to escape but that did not stop them complaining.

Unlike most of the other ranks in their camps, Captain Grant of the London Scottish found that when he arrived at Gütersloh Camp it was a pleasant surprise and far more comfortable than he had anticipated. He played soccer and hockey to help stay fit, he ate regular meals made from food sent from England, and was entertained by other officers in their quarters. Each day there was a camp news-sheet and monthly special editions. After two weeks in captivity the only thing he was able to gripe about in his diary was that wine and beer sales were to be stopped for a week because someone had got hold of an Austrian flag and hoisted it half-mast. However, within five days the ban was removed and he was able to celebrate his wedding anniversary. Unlike his men who were only allowed out of the camp on a work detail, he was allowed to leave the camp for a walk without an escort, just a guide. Officers gave their parole not to escape and walked around in large groups through the countryside and into the local towns.

Whereas other ranks could not count on the arrival of essentials, officers could. Captain Nobbs was 'impressed with the fair and systematic handling of ... parcels, letters, and money ... even letters and post-cards which arrived [after he had] been sent back to England were readdressed and sent back.'[50]

The better food, no work in poor conditions, regular exercise and greater freedom of movement meant that officers would stay healthier than the men. Plus officer camps had a visiting doctor so illness was picked up more quickly. For both officers and men, dental issues were dealt with outside the camp. Like Private Hall's visit to the dentist – an unforgettable experience – Captain Nobbs recorded that at Osnabrück camp 'the dentist was not a popular man to visit [because] he was apt to use his professional skill as an instrument to his patriotic ardour, and appeared to aspire to the removal of the jaw instead of the tooth.'[51]

One similarity with the rank-and-file prisoner was randomness of movement. After ten weeks of comfortable living Grant was warned he was moving camp. He was transferred to Crefeld Camp, for no particular reason he was aware of, where 'security was rigorous, with weekly searches for tunnelling'[52] and where in nine months there were twelve escape attempts, five of them successful.

Another similarity between both types of camp was roll call ('appell') on the appellplatz. For officers the procedure was less onerous especially at camps run by 'a professional soldier of the old school',[53] like that at Osnabrück where the com- mandant was a considerate, fair-minded gentleman. 'At Osnabrück the roll call was made by the officers simply parading outside of their respective rooms and coming to the salute as the German officer passed him, and he, in passing by, would answer the salute.'[54] There was no urgency, so officers tumbled out of bed a minute before roll call until full uniform was demanded. A solution to that problem was quickly found: parading in overcoats fitted the requirement.

Grant's diary entries make for an interesting comparison with the hard life of the ordinary soldier. After a short spell in his new camp he compared it with Gütersloh. On the whole he put his money on Gütersloh, principally because of the games. At Crefeld he could only get tennis and fives but the latter was full so he had to put his name on the very large waiting list. However, there were fifteen courts so he was able to play more than at Gütersloh, plus there was a loft converted into a gym where he could fence and box.

The food was better at Crefeld and there was a coffee bar where they were waited on by two buxom damsels, who to everyone's dismay disappeared when it was taken over by the officers. While other ranks had little or no money, even if they did there was little they could buy; but Grant could order what he wanted from the town through the dry canteen. Once again he was allowed out for a walk but this time through the town. Nobbs also found that he could buy anything he wanted, except food, through the obliging canteen manager.

While other ranks had to rely on themselves or their mates to get through, officers had orderlies – the polite name for a slave. However in those more class-ridden times, few saw anything wrong with it and when volunteers were asked for, many stepped forward. Relationships between batmen and officers in the trenches had been generally good and it was the same in camps, perhaps even better. They usually fared far better than those in enlisted men's camps because 'as a rule a strong bond of friendship developed between the officers and the orderlies, and a genuine interest was taken in' their welfare. 'An orderly need never be short of food or clothing (officers seemed to get unlimited supplies out from Britain).'[55]

In the camp an orderly looked after a number of officers in a variety of ways. They made beds, meals, tea, and performed general tidying up. Many performed an even more important function: assisting officers with their escape plans. 'The success of British officers in escaping the Kaiser's camps was due in great part to British orderlies.'[56] Indeed, one Corporal George McAllister was awarded the DCM for helping, at great personal expense and pain, officers to escape. He suffered a permanently damaged wrist protecting his head during a beating for helping an escape.

Life in an *Offizierlager* sounds idyllic in comparison to that in a *Mannschaftslager*, but they were still prisons, as Captain Nobbs described. 'A stroll around the building a few times, avoiding the barbed wire; or a few nights' sleep disturbed by the frequent challenge of the sentry and the barking of the watch-dogs'[57] would quickly dispel the idea that it was anything other than fettered captivity.

Although the numbers were small, British troops were taken prisoner by German forces in Africa. Conditions were the same in German South-West Africa where the prisoners were abused to make them look inferior in the eyes of the indigenous population. When British officers complained to the German Governor, Dr Seitz, he told them they should be grateful for what they got, adding, 'We did not invite you to this country. You invaded the country and fought us with natives.'[58] An official enquiry provided evidence that British prisoners were persistently starved. Like their fellow prisoners in Europe they were given short rations, placed in solitary confinement and treated harshly. Similarly, those who perpetrated the offences were not punished even though there was a loud outcry in South Africa for revenge.

Prisoners everywhere did not just sit back and accept their lot. They rebelled in a multitude of ways. There was graffiti: a portrait of the Kaiser in a urinal at Roubaix labour camp had the words 'WILHELM FUCK HIM'. They sang a wide range of songs. Men refused to salute German NCOs. They bated their captors, made fun of them by doing the goose-step, they skived and shirked work, acted mad, feigned illness, held go-slows, damaged, broke and sabotaged things, and set fire to them. And of course they escaped.

The inability of the Germans to punish officers for infractions made it easier for them to continue with indiscipline. 'Disorderly conduct on *Appell* became a standard protest.'[59] Officers shambled on to parade, turned up late, wore incorrect dress and refused to stay still while being counted. Although they were threatened by the armed guards, they felt secure enough to continue with their actions because they knew that the Germans were not prepared to put their own lives on the line by firing their weapons at officers. The guards were mostly old and unfit and knew that young fit officers might overpower them, that they might come off worst, and that certain members would be singled out for retribution.

Men tried to skive work in many ways. Those with long service chevrons turned them upside down and moved them up the arm to become senior NCOs; men above the rank of corporal were not supposed to labour. The danger was that they could end up in Minden or Grossenweidenmoor camps, notorious *Strafe* camps, as punishment. The most common skive was pretending to be sick. Unless the illness was unusual it was met with an aspirin and work or some form of violence. Strange and difficult-to-diagnose symptoms held more promise, especially if the illness appeared to be contagious. The most effective complaint, but one that could backfire and become real, was madness. Toothpaste could be used to fake an epileptic fit and chanting gibberish and covered yourself in dust or earth was a convincing symptom.

'Sabotage by PoWs in workplaces was carried out on an industrial scale, and if done slyly brought results for little risks.'[60] In the Roubaix vehicle repair depot the men 'put old screws and bits of metal off the workshop floor into the engine cylinders'[61] and while replacing one split pin would remove two. Working on a lock, Private Corker buried his tools or lost them in the river. Royal Marine Edward Page put six potatoes deep underground for every one he put in his basket. Punishment for such behaviour, although it could be severe – one man received ten years' detention in a civilian prison for putting sand instead of grease in a munitions factory cart – did not stop it.

At one camp they had burned the paper and cardboard from their Red Cross Parcels, scarce materials in Germany. In Holzminden they burned their German bread ration in front of their undernourished guards. Even with the war over they continued to get back at their captors. Before they finally left the camp in December 1918, they made one final snub at the Germans. Anything and everything that was combustible was used on a bonfire. 'It was a splendid sight and the Germans could only stand by helplessly, condemning the waste,'[62] noted one of the participants.

Notes

1. *The Times.*
2. Ibid
3. Nobbs, H.G.
4. Ibid.
5. *Reading Standard.*
6. *The Times History of the War, Volume XII.*
7. Ibid.
8. Ibid.
9. Ibid.
10. Ibid.
11. Ibid.
12. Ibid.
13. Ibid.
14. *The Times.*
15. Nobbs, H.G.
16. Hall, M.

17. Ibid.
18. van Emden, R.
19. *The Times.*
20. Ibid.
21. Hall, M.
22. Ibid.
23. Nobbs, H.G.
24. Ibid.
25. Hall, M.
26. *The Times.*
27. *The Times.*
28. van Emden, R.
29. Ibid.
30. Hall, M.
31. Ibid.
32. *Reading Standard.*
33. *The Times.*
34. Hall, M.
35. *The Times.*
36. Ibid.
37. Hall, M.
38. Nobbs, H.G.
39. Hall, M.
40. Ibid.
41. van Emden, R.
42. Nobbs, H.G.
43. Ibid.
44. Lewis-Stempel, J., *The War behind the Wire.*
45. van Emden, R.
46. Lewis-Stempel, J.
47. Ibid.
48. Nobbs, H.G.
49. Ibid.
50. Ibid.
51. Nobbs, H.G.
52. Moynihan, M., *Black Bread and Barbed Wire.*
53. Ibid.
54. Ibid.
55. Lewis-Stempel, J.
56. Lewis-Stempel, J.
57. Nobbs, H.G.
58. *The Times.*
59. Lewis-Stempel, J.
60. Lewis-Stempel, J.
61. Ibid.
62. Crawford, O.G.S., *Said and Done: The Auto-biography of an Archaeologist.*

An officers' barracks.

The food provided was insufficient and the arrival of parcels was always a welcome sight.

In most camps men were sent out on work parties – *arbeit kommando*. Here British prisoners are seen setting out for a day's work.

For most prisoners, if they could cope with the work, being on a farm was a relatively pleasant experience and one that provided extra food.

Work that might or might not have been forbidden under the conventions of PoW work. What would the wood be used for?

The caption for this picture was 'French prisoners still hungry after their meal'.

Prisoners died of disease, illness, accidents, brutality and some because they lost the will to live. A funeral for a camp member was an almost everyday occurrence in the bigger camps. Here Russian prisoners are burying a comrade.

Naturally no one took photographs of men searching through dustbins looking for anything edible so we have to rely on prisoner's testimony.

Serbian prisoners at Königsbrück Camp with their bagpipes.

In 1914, the French army wore uniforms not suited to twentieth century warfare. These are captured *Turcos* wearing bright clothing.

In the tented camp of Döberitz in 1915 there was little to do except hang around.

For those with money, some camps had a shop where it was possible to buy food and alcohol-free beer. In an officers' camp, the beer contained alcohol.

When the weather was nice the men could take exercise classes in the fresh air.

Inside the Russian Orthodox chapel at Zossen.

Russians mending shoes at Zossen Camp.

The Russian ward at Guben Camp was staffed by captured Russian medical staff.

Bringing in the clean bedding at Guben.

The French choir practising outdoors at Zossen Camp.

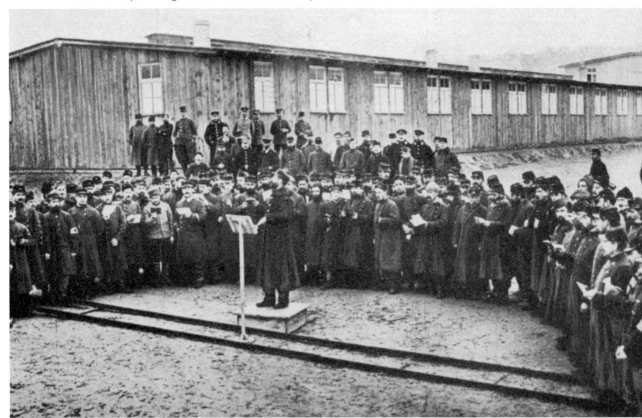

The funeral procession for a French major from Torgau, an officers' camp. The commandant of the Maubeuge fortress, General Fournier, was a prisoner there for the duration of the war.

A graveside ceremony for a British officer attended by a German band and camp officers.

Among the captured officers, there were men of high rank and others who were well known in their respective country. Some were deemed important because of their connections. This is Lieutenant Delcassé, son of the French Minister of the Exterior.

When there was little to do, men just sat around. Here they are joined by the camp's farm.

French North African cavalry at roll call.

The call to prayers at Crescent Camp.

A photo which could have appeared in the section on escape. Camps were patrolled by guards throughout the day. Here they are seen marching outside Clausthal Camp from where Kennard and Blain made an unsuccessful escape. The commandant, Heinrich Niemeyer, was the twin brother of Karl, commandant of Holzminden, scene of the great escape of the Great War.

Belgian prisoners waiting for their midday soup ration.

British prisoners at Döberitz eating their midday meal.

On arrival there was plenty of paperwork to complete.

To secure trenches, much wood was needed. Here British troops are shaping logs for trench walls.

Was this facility provided for other ranks as they convalesced? A wounded British officer dictating to a German Red Cross nurse a message for home.

Any employment that aided the war effort of the enemy was forbidden under the Geneva Convention. Here British troops are being employed in the construction of trenches. The trenches were in Germany – was this a contravention?

Scottish prisoners at Döberitz in late 1914.

Many prisoners found themselves responsible for constructing their own prison as numbers grew. Here French PoWs are constructing the fence to keep them inside.

A propaganda photograph to show how well the prisoners were fed: unloading large amounts of potatoes for the camp.

Some men could not wait to open their parcels.

Sport was a great way to forget your situation, relieve boredom and keep fit, if the facilities were provided. In some camps it was many months before any form of sport was possible but only then because equipment came from Britain.

Just as no one would photograph men scavenging from dustbins, there are no pictures other than an artist's representation of the way ill prisoners were treated at Langensalza. Reports stated that convalescents and suspected typhoid cases were put out in the rain while their clothes were being disinfected.

Accommodation in some of the early camps was primitive to say the least. This is Minden Camp in October 1914.

Soldiers on a work detail at Teltow, near Berlin, drawing their bread ration.

Blankenburg, in Brandenburg, was an officers' camp.

Having given their parole, officers were allowed out of the camp, accompanied, to enjoy walks, visit the local town, dine out and go shopping. Other ranks were shot if they tried to leave their camp.

WAR PRISONERS' CAMP, GIESSEN.

A WEEK'S BILL OF FARE. DAILY: 300 GRAMS OF BREAD.

Sunday.

Breakfast : Coffee and sugar.

	gr.
Coffee	5
Sugar	20

Dinner : Beef, potatoes and white cabbage.

Beef	120
Potatoes	750
White cabbage	300

Supper : Beans, starch meal, margarine and potatoes.

Field beans	100
Starch meal	20
Margarine	20
Potatoes	200

Monday.

Breakfast : Coffee and sugar.

Coffee	5
Sugar	20

Dinner : Bacon, potatoes and beans.

Bacon	30
Potatoes	750
Beans	150

Supper : Herring and potatoes.

One Herring	—
Potatoes	600

Tuesday.

Breakfast : Coffee and sugar.

Coffee	5
Sugar	20

Dinner : Pork, potatoes, and cabbage.

Pork	100
Potatoes	750
Cabbage	300

Supper : Beans, starch meal, margarine and potatoes.

Field beans	100
Starch meal	20
Margarine	20
Potatoes	200

Wednesday.

Breakfast : Potato-flour, starch meal and margarine.

Potato meal	30
Starch meal	60
Margarine	10

Dinner : Potato meal, potatoes, meat and vegetables.

	gr
Meat	30
Potato flour...	100
Potatoes	600
Dried vegetables	40

Supper : Rice, sugar and dried fruit.

Rice	100
Sugar	40
Dried fruit	50

Thursday.

Breakfast : Cocoa, sugar and starch meal.

Cocoa	30
Sugar	40
Amylum	20

Dinner : Salt meat, sauerkraut and potatoes.

Salt meat	100
Sauerkraut	250
Potatoes	600

Supper : Herring and potatoes.

One herring	—
Potatoes	600

Friday.

Breakfast : Coffee and sugar.

Coffee	5
Sugar	20

Dinner : Salt fish, potatoes and soup flavouring.

Salt fish	150
Potatoes	750
Soup flavouring	10

Supper : Cheese and potatoes.

Cheese	120
Potatoes	600

Saturday.

Breakfast : Potato-flour, starch meal and margarine.

Potato-flour...	30
Starch meal	60
Margarine	10

Dinner : Bacon, potatoes and beans.

Bacon	30
Potatoes	750
Beans	150

Supper : Rice, Sugar and Dried Fruit.

Dried fruit	50
Rice	100
Sugar	40

150—3

A week's menu at Giessen Camp. It differs markedly from the actual fare provided, according to prisoners statements.

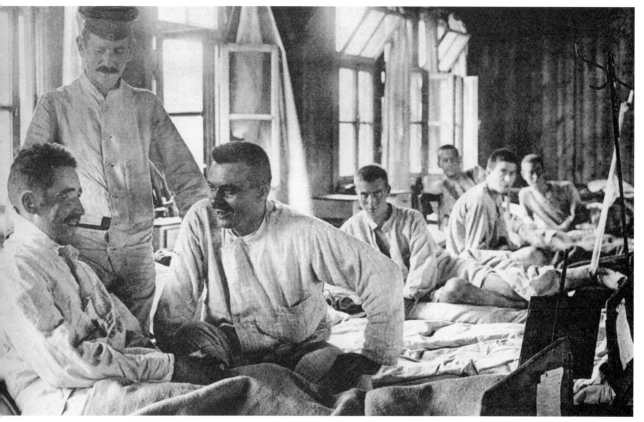

American prisoners in a German hospital.

A whole organisation developed to supply parcels to PoWs. This is the shop of the Hull PoWs committee where civilians and servicemen and women could buy goods to be sent to their nominated prisoner.

In their official books, the German authorities stressed the need for hygiene, comments which contradict some prisoner evidence and the written reports by neutral governments. This purports to show British troops at Baden Camp lined up to take a shower.

A view looking in to a standard-construction temporary camp. Two rings of wire indicate the shooting zone.

Around each camp were a series of watch towers; the size varied.

A year later at Minden Camp – tents.

Typical wooden huts at Puchheim.

Submariners pose outside their accommodation at Döberitz.

Inside the submariner's hut at Döberitz.

The inside of an enlisted men's barracks. According to many accounts, this is not what most men experienced.

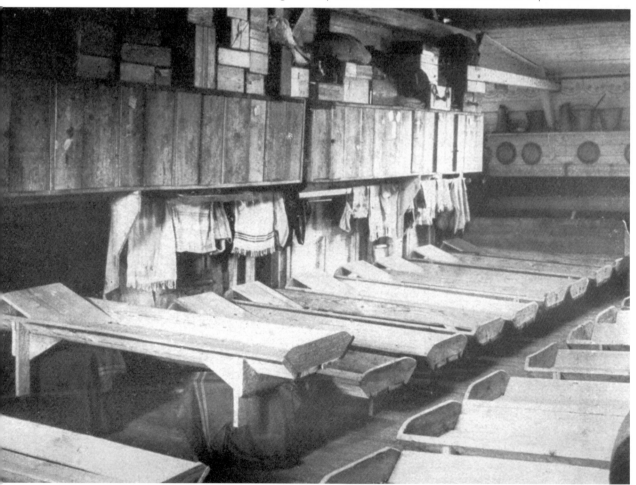

The idealised interior of a hut at Ebersdorf camp.

Men lined up for inspection – all seem to be in their best clothing.

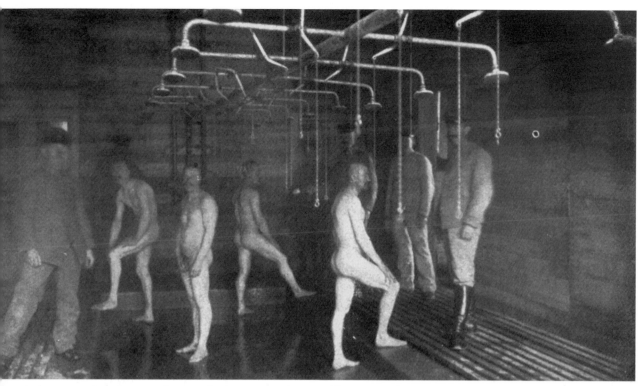

In better equipped camps the men had access to showers. The caption for this read: 'typical camp shower room'.

Disinfection tubs for newly arrived men at Königsbrück Camp.

Mobile clothes disinfecting apparatus.

An unlikely scenario: the commandant of Chemnitz camp is tasting the food prepared by Russian workers and a French chef.

In a perfect camp there was fresh bread every day – here being inspected by the camp officials.

Preparing food followed strict religious and racial segregation.

A propaganda photo to show how much coal and how many potatoes were available at Merseburg Camp.

These PoWs have been to collect their parcels and transport them to the camp for distribution.

The distribution of parcels in a French barracks.

French PoWs relaxing in the leisure room at Giessen Camp.

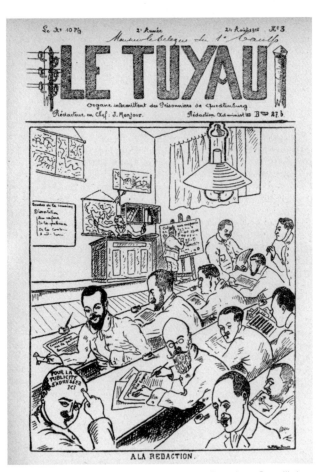

The French camp newspaper produced at Quedlinburg and the Russian camp newspaper produced at Döberitz.

Camp personnel as guests to an evening of light entertainment provided by the French theatre group at Dyrotz.

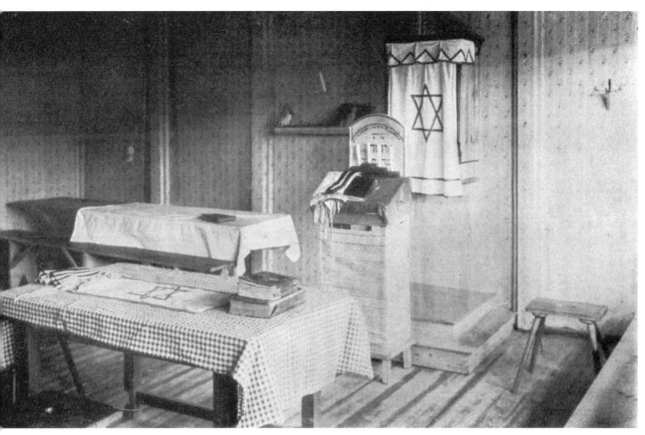

There were many men of the Jewish faith fighting on both sides. This is the synagogue at Frankfurt an der Oder.

When sufficient instruments and players were available, a camp orchestra was formed. Having an orchestra meant that the thespians in the camp could perform musicals.

In the better camps prisoners were encouraged to provide their own food to supplement rations.

Keeping livestock was encouraged to supplement food supplies.

Prisoners at Brandenburg Camp were allowed to bathe in the Havel during the summer months.

In what appear to be comfortable barracks, French prisoners relax after work.

An officer's room at Königstein. The camp was in the fortress and held only French and Russian PoWs.

The hospital at Dyrotz Camp.

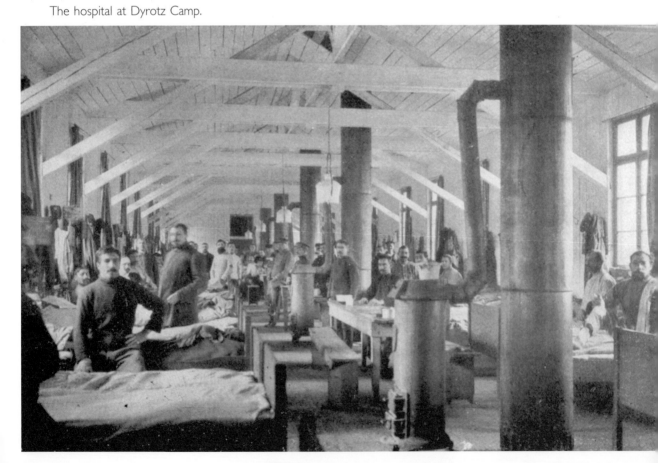

A view of the lake and officer villas at the Neubrandenburg Camp.

Crescent Camp showing prayers during a Muslim festival.

Not all the men captured were Christian. In order to persuade non-white prisoners that they should rise up against their colonial masters, they were generally well treated. This is the Crescent Camp at Wünsdorf showing sheep slaughtering at Beiram festival, probably Eid.

An aerial view of Giessen camp showing its proximity to the town. Note the tram in the bottom right.

The medical centre at Schwäbisch Gmünd.

A view of the terrace at Helmstedt officers' camp.

Camps in the countryside could look very pleasant, like this in Schwäbisch Gmünd, a town in Baden-Württemberg.

At a PoW collection point, British troops happily wait to move to their new homes. Although there are a number of Germans in the photo, only one is on guard.

Two very young Russian prisoners
held at Stendal Camp.

Officers' quarters in Mainz Camp.

An officer's room at Rosenberg-Kronach Camp which was located in Festung Rosenberg, above the town of Kronach. Charles de Gaulle was held as a PoW there.

Officers' drawing room at Karlsruhe.

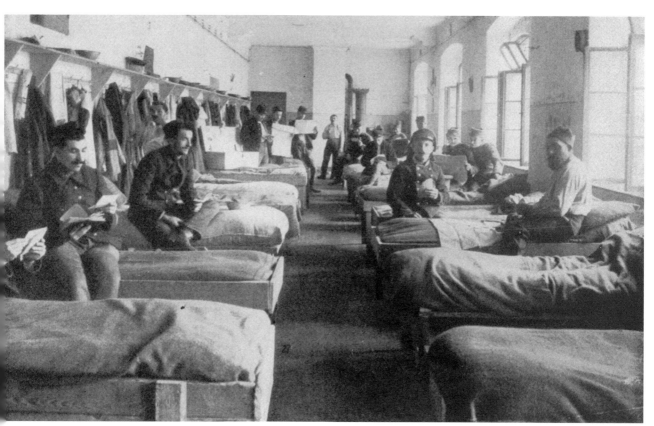

Soldiers' accommodation in a Stuttgart barracks.

The very elaborate hairdressing salon at Münster Camp.

Once the food was prepared it was placed in large tureens and picked up by members of the different barracks. This orderly queue was photographed at Langensalza Camp.

At Münster, pig farming was encouraged.

Keeping rabbits helped supplement food supplies.

French first-aiders at Heuberg Camp. As most German medical personnel were needed by the army, in many camps much of the medical care was provided by captured male nurses. Note the clogs being worn; usually when there were no boots available.

English officers showing off their pets. Officers had enough space, time and spare food to look after a dog.

Gardening was encouraged at Stendal Camp.

At Stuttgart Camp some of the prisoners were trained as firemen.

At Friedrichsfeld Camp the men were provided with basket-making materials.

The linen sorting and mending room at Giessen.

As with musicians, a large group will always have some who love to write. Many camps set up their own magazines and newspapers. This is the typesetting room for the paper *L'Echo de Camp de Rennbahn* (*The Racecourse Camp Echo*). The paper was produced in Münster Camp.

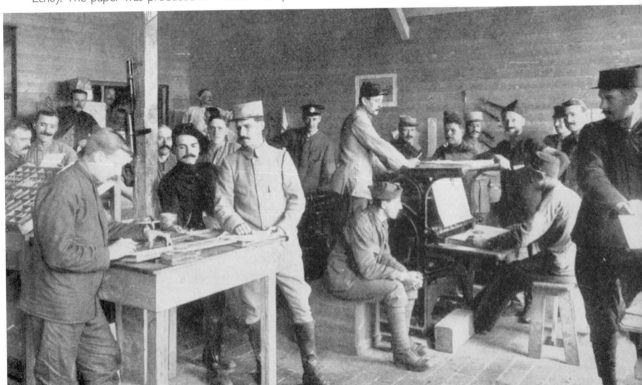

When timber was available men could make things to improve their own life or to sell. This is the joiner's shop at Frankfurt an der Oder Camp.

The spotless operating theatre in Hameln Camp.

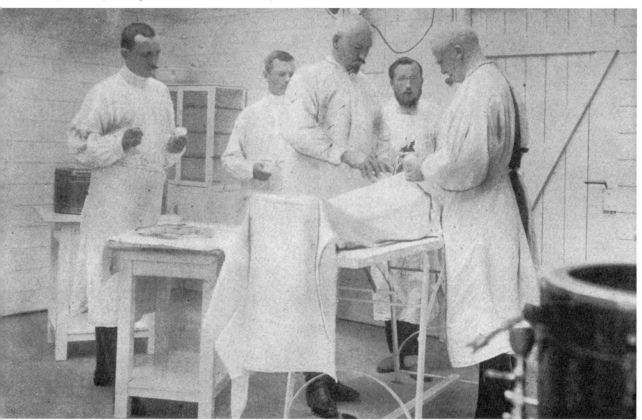

A German doctor inoculating Russian prisoners at Frankfurt Camp.

A summer picnic.

Something not usually mentioned in PoW accounts of their time in captivity: an outside gymnasium.

Officers were provided with vastly superior leisure spaces and equipment. Here Romanian officers are enjoying a game of billiards at Crefeld.

National differences were apparent when it came to games. Boccia uses leather balls, therefore it was not dangerous, so it was an ideal substitute for the more favoured game of Pétanque.

The sculptor for the Güstrow memorial was a French prisoner, seen here at work.

Some camps had extensive libraries. Parchim Camp had an extensive library just for Flemish speakers.

On arrival parcels were placed in a secure building. The distribution was controlled by the camp guards who usually checked parcels for contraband. In some cases they withheld them as punishment. Here they are being distributed to the camp populace by delivery men.

A Jewish religious service in the Frankfurt synagogue.

Christmas gift time at Bautzen Camp, accompanied by music. What gifts they would have had access to, as they are mostly Russian, will never be known.

Christmas at Trier, a hospital camp. Although it looks nice and cosy, none of the men looks especially pleased. Perhaps it was a propaganda photograph.

The memorial in the cemetery at Güstrow.

NO. 2.   THE UNVEILING OF MEMORIAL STONE, PARCHIM, NOV., 1918.

Before being released the men of Parchim Camp unveiled a memorial stone to the men who would not be returning home.

The funeral of an obviously well-respected British PoW. At some camps the cemetery was outside the camp fencing so the cortege had to be escorted to the burial ground. This was taken at Sprottau, a camp 3 miles from the town, and also a *Lazarett* for prisoners with tuberculosis.

A graveside service for a British PoW.

The type of work provided by a camp depended on its location. Men in camps close to industrial areas would most likely do factory or mining work – the least pleasant. Those in the countryside might do a variety of jobs. Here French prisoners are constructing a building – probably for non-military use.

Gefangene Franzosen
An der Arbeit

Russian PoWs setting out for a day cleaning the streets.

A French work detail outside the camp. After a return to the main camp the sender of this card told his family that he was glad to be back with them as it was nicer than the camp.

A Christmas frieze in a PoW church.

The altar of a catholic church in an unknown camp.

Poking fun at their guards with a giant snowman, French prisoners appear to be having fun despite a lack of freedom.

Religion was important to many of the men. Camps provided religious spaces in buildings and some built new churches. This is the newly built church for Cottbus Camp. Above the door reads 'Glory to God in the highest'.

The camp at Giessen had a church hall just for Irish men.

Athletics was a popular summer activity, with equipment provided from England.

Group 5 British football team in 1918 pose in front of the Red Cross quarters in an unknown camp.

In an attempt to keep boredom at bay, art was a popular pastime. This is an art exhibition in an unknown camp.

What this occasion was is not recorded, other than in 1916 the French prisoners held a carnival at Puchheim Camp. Perhaps it was their 14 July celebration.

The French theatre group at Cottbus Camp.

Quite where they managed to get such a range of costumes from may never be known. This was a New Year's fancy dress dance held at Döberitz.

As in other-ranks camps, officers also entertained each other with music and theatrical productions.

Every large group of people contains some who are musical. When instruments arrived from home, ad hoc musical groups formed. This band appears to comprise British, French and Russian players.

The officers' Pierrot troupe at Mainz Camp.

Most camps had a large building that could double as a theatre that would normally be full for every performance.

The potato-peeling army at Cottbus Camp.

Prison life was regimented, with regular inspections and roll calls.

Two French prisoners, both wearing wooden shoes, are putting the finishing touches to an artistic construction in the roll call area, watched by a senior member of the Guard Company.

The hospital bandaging room at Güstrow.

As it should have been but more likely a propaganda photo of French style bread making.

The reality of most PoW kitchens. Individual barrack food containers are placed on the floor ready for distribution.

French mail with a guard in control. Along with the parcels, letters were an important part of a prisoner's life, showing that people cared.

Playing cards was a popular pastime, mostly for fun but some men made considerable amounts of money during their stay.

A canteen where the men could buy hot drinks and alcohol-free beer.

Each prisoner had their own eating utensils which they looked after carefully. Here prisoners are getting their midday meal.

The communal reading and writing room in Mainz Camp.

The arrival of parcels generated great interest.

A MERRY CHRISTMAS

FROM .... No. ....

OFFIZIER - GEFANGENENLAGER
STRALSUND (DÄNHOLM) BAR .... STUBE ....

Date..191

1. Have you received your parcels up to date? If not, which have you missed?

2. What is number and date of the last received?

3. Were contents in good condition?

4. Do you wish any change made in any standard parcel?

5. Please give your <u>full</u> address on the other side of this card.

Signature...

It is most essential that the receipt of this parcel should be acknowledged.

A Christmas card produced for December 1918 by the officers at Stralsund Camp; it was never needed.

In order to track their parcels, recipients were provided with a card to fill in.

A postcard drawn by Seaman Cecil Tooke during his stay at Döberitz.

DOEBERITZ   JAN 1915

ALWAYS MERRY & BRIGHT

Probably a photo by German authorities for racial stereotyping – would the man have had his photo taken like that to send home?

A Russian soldier photographed for racial analysis.

Three British soldiers who have paid for the privilege of having their photo taken show they have little to smile about.

If all the guards were not very nice why have your photo taken with one? Two Russians and a guard. As the reverse of the card is in Russian it is probable they were there voluntarily.

A cheerful keepsake of their time in captivity. From right to left: E. Monkman, 2/5th London; Dr David Goldenberg (Russian Colonel); Self (unknown RFC pilot); Dr I. Rubetski (Russian Captain) and I.P. Ivens, 14th Warwicks from Small Heath.

The Germans were keen photographers of the different racial and ethnic groups they captured. This happy, fine-looking soldier, is from Senegal.

A lancer escorting two Russian soldiers, both of whom had time to get their blankets before moving.

Celebrating with a glass of wine. Christmas was a far more cheery time in an officers' camp.

Prisoners had red bands put on their uniforms or clothing; the Frenchman on the left also has the letters KG (*Kriesgefangener* – PoW) painted on his tunic.

Relatively few religious ministers were made prisoner so a German priest often stood in to deal with spiritual needs.

A captured padre, who could probably have been exchanged, is shown here with two of the prisoners.

On arrival at the camp prisoners had to be processed. Here they are queuing to get through the inner entrance.

New prisoners being taken into the interior of the camp before being detailed to the various blocks.

In many camps the local photographer was allowed in to take photographs of the inmates, if they could afford to pay. This is Seaman Wheel who survived the Battle of Jutland.

Officers went through the same entry process as the men, but as there were fewer of them it was considerably quicker. These officers were captured during the Spring Offensive and are being processed at Karlsruhe Camp.

Parcels had to be packed in a certain way or they were likely not to arrive.

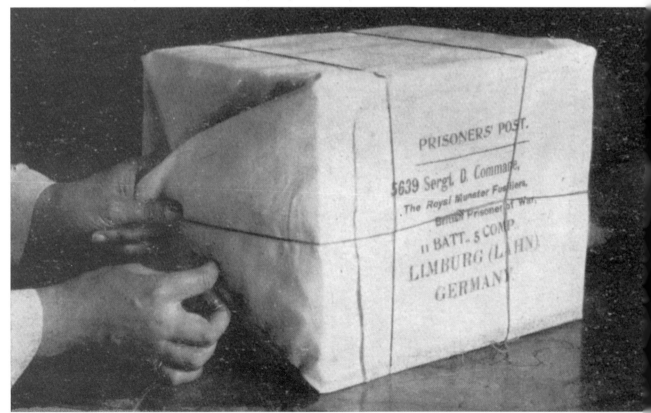

Typical contents of a parcel sent from home.

Chapter Four

Escape

Some prisoners made the most of any disturbance to break free. While Brigade Major Howitt was being escorted to the rear by two guards a British shell exploded close by. Finding his captors had hidden in a shell-hole he attacked the first one to get up, smashed him into the second, and then rolled them into a ditch. Gathering his wits, he ran for it. Fortunately they were poor shots and although they emptied their revolvers at him he was not hit. He kept running until nightfall when he found that there were outposts nearby. Expecting them to be German he was about to risk it all on a dash between two of the posts when he heard a 'single familiar Anglo-Saxon syllable, uttered in a tone of deep disgust, but it was music to Howitt's ears for it could only have come from the lips of a British Tommy. He could have wept with relief.'[1] His only remaining problem was to convince them he was British.

For most there was no chance to escape before being moved back. However, the possibility of escape would be something, that for many, would keep their spirits up while passing their time in captivity.

Escape was not just for officers, enlisted men also tried and succeeded. In April 1917, three men of the Dorsets who had been captured and presumed dead arrived in British lines. After their capture they had been made to work within firing distance of the lines, poorly fed, given no clothing and their communications home had been destroyed. No one knew they existed. At Sauchy-Cauchy they had been housed in a disused brick kiln. Seizing their chance one night, they dropped to the ground, slipped past the guards and headed towards the gun flashes. They managed to cross the German lines and made it to their own trenches. To demonstrate their poor treatment it was recorded that one of the men had weighed thirteen stone at the time of his capture but was only eight stone when he crossed in to British lines.

Once in a camp, escape opportunities had to be carefully planned as in most cases the men did not know exactly where they were. But the plan did not have to be complicated, as evidenced by the first man to escape from Westerholt Camp and get to England. Private Macdonald of the Gordon Highlanders simply ran out of the ranks as his party was marching to the mine one morning at 6.00am and made his getaway. Fortunately the guards were too astonished to fire.

This escape encouraged others to try their luck and soon recaptured escapees were kept apart from the others. Known to the Germans as the 'Bad men's party', they were treated worse than other prisoners. Members freely exchanged information gained during their escape attempts in the hope that it would enable one of the party to make a 'Home Run'. Rifleman Evanson duly joined the party and eventually succeeded in making it back home where the army put him in the accountancy section.

On 31 May 1917, a Hull soldier arrived home unexpectedly: Private Samuel Blackshaw, who had worked for Messrs G. Brown, shipbuilders, before the war. He had volunteered on 7 September 1914 and gone to France in April 1915 where he was made a PoW. After being sent to four camps, he eventually escaped.

Some men made more than one attempt; indeed, seven men are recorded as having tried five or more times. The champion escaper was Second Lieutenant Medlicott, RFC, who escaped fourteen times but unfortunately did not make it home. He was allegedly shot while attempting to escape on the journey from the railway station back to his camp after recapture.

Owing to the severity of their treatment, many Russians tried to escape and considerable numbers made it. Unknown numbers, probably hundreds, escaped from *Arbeitskommando* on the Western Front; a risky business as an escaper could get shot at by both sides during the attempt. They could also be executed, as were four British soldiers who killed a German soldier when he discovered their hiding place.

It is not possible to provide an exact number for attempted escapes. The official figures for British and Empire escapers is: 54 officers and 519 other ranks. A total of 573 men made a 'Home Run' of whom nearly half had already made two previous attempts. Uta Hinz[2] suggests that there were 313,400 escape attempts during the war and that 67,565 succeeded (this total includes all Allied escapers).

Eventually the British Army realised the importance of escapers in providing information. As a result escape was encouraged by the sending of practical aid: compasses, maps and wire-cutters were just some of the articles sent, hidden in food parcels, and after the war many of the escapers were decorated.

A successful escape needed good planning, resources, and luck. Things often went wrong. Structures collapsed making a tunnel unsafe, subsidence revealed the tunnel or affected structures around it, tunnels flooded, the weather changed unexpectedly, guard routines changed suddenly, guards became suspicious and searched more thoroughly, or appeared when not expected.

While careful planning was usually a prerequisite for success, chance could also play its part. While moving camp was an upheaval it did provide a chance of escape. *The Times* of 16 April 1917 carried a story about an officer who escaped when he was being transferred to a new camp. Moving at night, hiding by day, coming perilously close to being discovered three times, he was eventually stopped by a guard. As his papers were apparently in order he was allowed on his way and, after walking through the unguarded border, was in Holland.

Potential escapers also had to watch out for stoolies. One breakout was foiled by a German posing as a Russian officer, another by an orderly with Sinn Fein leanings. Sometimes it was another officer: at Osnabrück an officer was 'covered in treacle, excrement and cold water'[3] for betraying an escape attempt.

Many and varied were the ways in which men tried to escape, with officers having a greater range of possibilities. Dressing as a German soldier or officer required special clothing but dressing as a workman was more straightforward. Evans details just a few methods of escape used by the men in Fort 9: hiding in a dirty-clothing basket; hiding in a muck tub and being wheeled out of camp; swimming across a moat camouflaged with green paint; tunnelling; cutting the wire; making a bridge from the castle building to the wall and simply jumping off the end.

Once again officers were at an advantage when it came to planning and provisioning. While most other ranks received little enough food anyway without being able to build up a store to help on an escape run, officers, as has been previously mentioned, received regular parcels. The extra food was a great help, but what was contained in it might have been more important.

Captain Evans, a reconnaissance pilot who had been shot down on 16 July 1916, wrote about his time in captivity in *The Escaping Club*. Like Rifleman Evanson, he was moved from one camp to another, first Gütersloh, then to Clausthal. After his failed escape attempt he was put with other attempted escapees in Fort 9 at Ingolstadt where it is estimated that three-quarters were scheming to escape. Of the 150 officers in the camp, at least 130 had successfully broken out of other camps and stayed free for up to three weeks before their eventual recapture. Fort 9 was the officers' version of Evanson's 'Bad men's party' and like the enlisted men they also pooled their knowledge and were ready to help each other escape. They did not worry about the consequences and most had done a spell in solitary confinement. Evans did eventually escape, in the summer of 1917. After recuperation and retraining he was sent to Palestine where his engine failed and he was captured, this time by the Turks.

Two other *Strafe* camps were just as bad as Ingolstadt: Holzminden and Ströhen. 'The latter was literally riddled with tunnels, and held the record for the biggest number of successful escapes.'[4]

It was easier for officers to receive materials that could assist any escape attempt. Evans described how easy it was to smuggle contraband into the escapers' camp and to get messages to the men. 'Watching a German open a parcel in which you knew there was a concealed compass is quite one of the most amusing things I have ever done. Most of the maps came baked in the middle of cakes which I received weekly from home, and as I was on comparatively good terms with the Germans who searched our parcels, they used to hand these over to me without ever probing them. One of the compasses came in a glass bottle of prunes … a second compass came in a small jar of anchovy paste … I remember decoding one postcard from my mother, and making out the message to be "Maps in Oswego". But what was Oswego? No one had any idea.'[5] It turned out to be the name of a brand of flour that his mother had sent him. He felt lucky to have got all the things safely, particularly when the whole of the crust on one of his cakes was composed entirely of maps. Fortunately the baking had browned the oil-paper in which they were sewn so that it looked exactly like cake.

Messages could be hidden in anything. One officer regularly received dried fruit for his health but when this private store was raided to provide dessert for the others, messages were found floating in the stewed fruit being prepared. Instead of a stone, each prune had a message.

Officers also had money. At Clausthal camp, a local tailor came in to do repairs. During 1915 he had brought in to the camp a number of civilian suits and sold them to the officers. When the Germans found this out they tried to confiscate them but naturally none was found. So when Captain Evans decided to escape it was relatively easy for him to come by the necessary civilian clothing. In an officers' camp, money could buy essentials for an escape, not that the Germans intended to assist escape.

Osnabrück Camp sold a manicure set with nail clippers strong enough to cut perimeter wire. Many of the officers' canteens sold oil cloth, and matches. Holz-minden 'sold children's printing kits which were ideal for forging identity cards, birth certificates and travel permits.'[6] At Fort Zorndorf, the manufacture of escape materials was almost on an industrial scale. Each week there was a secret market at which escape requisites were sold: clothing, maps, documents, compasses. What could not be bought, stolen, bartered or smuggled in had to made in the camp, so many men became proficient tailors. It was the same at Neuenkirchen where 'the prisoners had organized a veritable escape factory in a small room at the top of the house' where 'all sorts of escape kit were manufactured.'[7] The noise of any hammer-ing was drowned out by a Wimshurst machine they had manufactured and was continually making static electricity while they worked.

Unless promoted from the ranks, most officers were well educated and able to speak at least a little of some foreign language. For those who intended to escape from Germany, their schoolboy German was a boon, and many spent a considerable amount of time making it sound less schoolboy. After all, if you were going to travel by train you had to buy a ticket and you may have to speak to someone at some point. A few choice phrases could suffice, as Captain Evans found at the station in Düsseldorf when he bought a plan of the city. The vendor insisted on discussing 'the weather, the war and the increase of paper money with every new war loan.'[8] By confining his remarks to basic replies, '"*Ja wünderschön,*" "*Da haben Sie recht,*" "*Ja wohl,* es *geht nicht so schlimm*," "*Kolossal*"," he survived the encounter and passed as a German. Their education and training also gave them confidence — essential when things did not go according to plan.

Evans lost his travelling partner and, feeling he was being watched at the station, decided to go for a walk around the city, coming back regularly to check if his partner had arrived. The plan had been to find a Dutch barge on the river and get a lift. Without a partner he changed the plan. Purchasing a map of Crefeld, after much discussion about spies, he eventually caught a tram across the Rhine and another tram to Crefeld where he made his way to the Dutch border. Within yards of freedom he was caught and sent back.

Recaptured escapees were held under armed guard and escorted back by train — a possibly unpleasant journey for an other-ranker but not so for an officer as Evans recalled. Although told he would be shot if he attempted to escape he was treated courteously and fed well. On the train, when he gave his parole not to escape, the escort put their weapons on the rack and then got a bag containing food and wine. On his return his punishment was fourteen days in 'a very nasty, bare, whitewashed brick room, next to the pigsties.'[9] He was allowed to have food, tobacco and books sent to him and there was a bed, a basin and a stove. Evans says it was a fairly uncomfortable time but to an other-ranker it would have been paradise.

Escapers had to be bold and physically fit as they could be walking across difficult terrain for long periods with little to sustain them. One of the longest escapes was made by a Canadian, Private Drope, who broke out of Heilsberg Camp in East Prussia on 13 June 1918 with two Russians. His 500-mile trip to freedom in Russia took five weeks. Probably the honour for the longest time taken to get to freedom goes to Lieutenant O'Brien, an American serving with the RFC. He jumped from a train near Strasburg on 9 September 1917 and headed for Holland. 'After a journey of seventy-two days'[10] he reached Holland.

Even with careful planning, unexpected changes and bad luck meant that most attempts would fail. Evans recorded some of the failures in *The Escape Club*. After three weeks of 'skilful labour in making a hole through 4 feet of masonry,'[11] it was discovered by the guards when it was almost finished. A bar-cutting attempt was foiled at the last minute. Evans worked on a tunnel, in air so bad the candle would not stay lit. The gallery was so tight that anyone working on it had to lie on their front and pull themselves along. It was planned to open out the tunnel above the frozen moat and then disappear in to the night but a thaw came and plans had to be changed. As they waited for the right weather conditions, their luck ran out and a liquid-filled depression appeared above their tunnel. Once prodded with bayonets the game was up.

Most escapes involved at most a handful of men, but the breakout from Holzminden camp, a cavalry barracks built in 1913, was the site of the original great escape. In July 1918, twenty-nine officers escaped through a tunnel, ten of whom evaded recapture and managed to get back to Britain. The camp was opened in September 1917 to house between 500 and 600 British and British Empire officers and their orderlies, many of whom came from an overcrowded smaller camp in the *X.Armee Korps* area. Initially it was commanded by a kindly elderly officer, but he was soon replaced by a Captain Niemeyer who remained commandant until the end of the war. This commandant had a reputation for cruelty. His vindictiveness and apparent pleasure in making life difficult for the officers earned the camp the epithet 'Hellzminden'. His twin brother was commandant at Clausthal camp.

The camp held a number of prisoners who were notable at the time and some who would be in the future. Among them were: three Victoria Cross winners, Edward Donald Bellew, Edward Bingham and William Leefe Robinson; Michael Claude Hamilton Bowes-Lyon, son of the 14th Earl of Strathmore and Kinghorne, and brother of the future Queen Elizabeth, the Queen Mother; James Whale, Hollywood film director to be; Brian Horrocks, an important Second World War British Army general; two victims of the Red Baron: Christopher Guy Gilbert (31st victim) and Algernon Frederick Bird (61st victim).

Preparations for the escape began in November 1917, using spoons, sharpened cutlery and tools stolen from the camp to dig the tunnel. Bed slats were used to shore it. 'They designed and made an ingenious ventilation system, fake uniforms and official papers.'[12] This was not the first attempt from the camp but certainly the most famous. From the first days, numerous attempts had been made, many were successful but few escapees remained at large for more than a few days.

Their initial plan was a short tunnel but this was stopped when a guard became suspicious. The next tunnel was much longer and took about nine months to complete. While some stood guard over the tunnel entrance concealed under a staircase in the orderlies' quarters, thirteen men took it in turns to dig. They were to be the first to escape and the rest would follow. Escape was to take place on the night of 23/24 July 1918.

Of the men who planned to escape, only twenty-nine succeeded because the tunnel collapsed, leaving many more waiting for the turn that never came. The three main diggers were friends and they all made it safely to Holland with the one who spoke fluent German acting as guard for the other two, one of whom pretended to be insane. A further seven made it back to England, one of whom was the senior British officer in the camp, Colonel Charles Rathborne, a fluent German speaker who travelled quickly by train to Aachen and then walked the 3 miles to the Dutch border. Of the ten successful escapers, seven were members of the air force. The remaining nineteen were recaptured.

This was the single biggest breakout through a tunnel during the war but there were others. On 18 August 1916 nineteen officers escaped from Torgau, in May

1918 twenty-four men escaped from Schweidnitz, and in September 1918 sixteen escaped from Graudenz.

Escape was probably on most men's mind at some time during their captivity. Private Tucker, a man who sabotaged German vehicles in Roubaix, stated: 'escape was never far from our thoughts, whatever the circumstances.'[13] But comparatively few tried it and indeed some thought those that did try were foolish. In his diary Rifleman Hall simply recorded the failed attempt of a Canadian who was caught after two days of freedom. A friend, Private Clarke, felt differently: 'Holland of the Canadians made a fool of himself by trying to escape, roughly forty hours before being caught, had managed to wander 4 kilometres during that time being found in the next village.'[14]

Why did so few try to escape? Captain Nobbs had contact with many men during his captivity and when he asked why they did not try to escape, especially as they were on farms, he received a very simple answer: 'While the work was hard they preferred it; as they lived with the farmer, who treated them well if they worked well. They ate at the farmer's table, and had no non-commissioned officers to bully them; whereas, if they attempted to escape and were caught they would be sent to work in the mines or other equally unpopular task.'[15]

Perhaps more obviously, most would not know how to navigate their way across Germany; the majority of escapers would be doomed to failure and the resulting poor treatment that would follow. The punishment was based on German military law, in which escape was technically punishable by death. An escape broke many regulations and the resulting punishment was often unduly severe in British eyes. Nominal sentences of days could become weeks and months.

For many officers it was their duty to escape, so they tried. Lieutenant Hardy made ten attempts. In most officer camps it was the natural choice, but not in all, especially in more comfortable camps like Friedburg. There was some antipathy to escape among older officers and often among pre-war regulars. 'The Senior British Officer at Torgau, Colonel W.E. Gordon, straightforwardly ordered PoWs not to escape in autumn 1914; when one officer disappeared, his absence was reported to the camp authorities.'[16] Escaping was frowned upon at Clausthal. The commandant was Heinrich Niemeyer, twin of Karl, commandant at Holzminden. The SBO at Clausthal, Brigadier Ravenshaw, even went as far as to threaten new arrivals with court martial if they attempted to escape. Most went along with the no-escape rule because Niemeyer punished those in the camp after an escape, even if they were not involved.

At Magdeburg in 1916, escape was not for gentlemen, and anyway 'why bother?' was the general feeling. After all, as a result of talks, officers who had been in captivity for more than thirty months could move to a neutral country for the duration. But this did not entirely stop attempts to escape.

Regardless of the dangers involved and even with the war drawing to its end, men still thought of escape, for whatever reason: it would tie down German troops, they could not stand being a prisoner any longer, or because it was their patriotic duty. Plans continued to be made even though failure could mean a bullet in the back at any moment or electrocution on the fences surrounding the Dutch border. Ernie Stevens and Sid Stockwell took that chance. In late September they escaped from the factory they worked in and almost made it to the Dutch border. On their capture, one guard told them they would be home by Christmas because Germany was finished. In October 1918 an American naval officer escaped to Switzerland. And on 9 November an escaper was returned to his camp where the commandant told him not to escape because the war would be over in two days.

Notes

1. MacDonald, L.
2. Hinz, U., *Gefangen im Großen Krieg. Kriegsgefangenschaft in Deutschland 1914–1921*.
3. Lewis-Stempel, J.
4. Jackson, R., *The Prisoners 1914–18*.
5. Evans, A.J., *The Escaping Club*.
6. Lewis-Stempel, J.
7. Jackson, R.
8. Evans, A.J.
9. Ibid
10. Jackson, R.
11. Evans, A.J.
12. Lewis-Stempel, J.
13. Lewis-Stempel, J.
14. Hall, M.
15. Nobbs, H.G.
16. Ibid'.

Hauptmann Karl Niemeyer, notorious commandant of Holzminden Camp which was famous for its great escape. 'Milwaukee Bill', as he was known, spoke a version of American English which resulted in him being ridiculed by the prisoners. Discipline in the camp was often arbitrary and punitive. Atrocities were allegedly committed, which included the bayoneting of prisoners.

A view of Kaserne B at Holzminden from where the great escape started.

The view from Kaserne B at Holzminden, an officer's camp, showing the town, the relatively low wire fence and the ice rink made in January 1918. The camp held 500–600 officer prisoners and approximately 100–160 other-ranks prisoners. These men acted as officers' servants and performed other tasks around the camp.

The track of the Holzminden tunnel after it had been dug up.

The mouth of the Holzminden tunnel.

Orderlies digging out the tunnel between Kaserne B and the outer wall.

A group of recaptured officers in a room at Holzminden. Left to Right: Churchill, Lyon, Clouston, Robertson, Sharp, Bennet and Matlock.

The majority of escape attempts failed for a range of reasons. For those that got close to the border there was a final danger, an electric fence. Here guards are removing the remains of a dead cat from the wire using an insulated hook. The warning on the high tension wire between Belgium and Holland read, 'Warning: High tension. Dangerous to life', with a guard house behind in case anyone successfully crossed the wires.

An escapee who was electrocuted.

As well as having an electric fence, some sections of the border were especially tightly guarded.

Most parcels were checked for contraband. A compass was found in this bread roll from France.

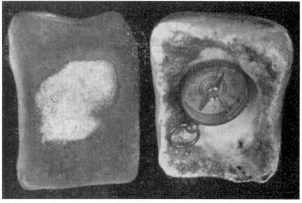

These were found in a tin contained in a box from France – a rubber band and rubber balloon; purpose unknown.

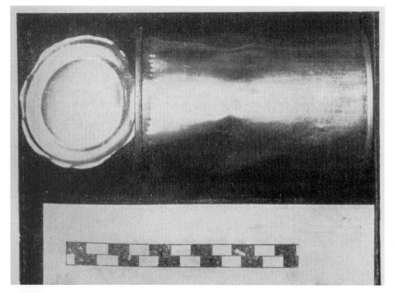

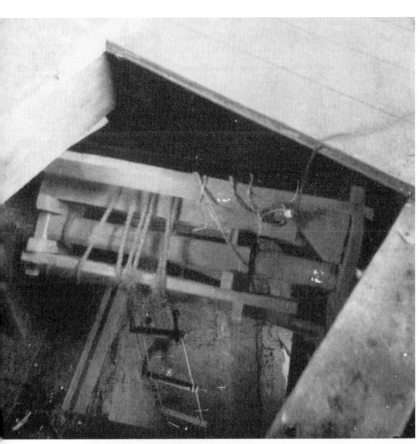

Under the floor of the French camp adjutant's room at Zwickau Lager, the guards discovered a manhole with a rope ladder.

This photograph shows the end of the tunnel from the adjutant's room, in Zwickau Camp.

Digging and ventilation equipment for the tunnel dug at Zwickau.

Chapter Five

Civilian Internees

The internment of enemy aliens occurred in all the combatant nations, to a lesser or greater extent. All nations immediately interned enemy aliens of combatant age; what happened to other groups varied according to country and year. What happened to individual families also varied according to circumstances and perception. Internment was seen as a way of preventing internal problems, of removing spies and other dangerous individuals, and of showing the public they were being protected. In Britain many wanted it to go a step further and for those with enemy surnames to be interned, even if they were naturalised. This led to some strange situations. In Hull, many wanted the pork butcher Hohenrein interned, even though he had been born in Britain, and his son had served in the army. Over in Germany his son was interned as being British. All aliens had to be registered, but what to do if they didn't and joined the British Army under an alias? In Berkshire one did and became a sergeant before he was discovered; he was discharged from service just before he was to be sent overseas.

There were relatively few British and French nationals in Germany when the war started, official police figures gave the total as 10,168. As they were not seen as a security threat, all they needed to do was obey a curfew order and report to their local police station once a week. When mobilisation had finished, men over military age, and women and children, were allowed to leave the country. In total there were around 1.2 million foreigners in Germany at the start of the war of which 50,000 were Russian.

When war seemed inevitable some rushed to leave the country taking only what they could fit in a suitcase. Most, like Isaac Cohen, stayed. He was on holiday in Schandau where the walls were plastered with patriotic proclamations. Here the police hunted for the rumoured Russian spies in the district. Cohen was picking up his mail when a policeman asked him for his papers, asked if he was Russian, and then informed him that his passport, British and issued in Berlin, wasn't German. Escorted to the Town Hall his papers were checked by the baker, the only person who understood English, and although suspected of being a Russian spy by his escort was allowed to leave. Nearby, workmen had discovered a man dressed as a woman who they believed was also a Russian spy. On examination by the doctor's wife she turned out to be female. When war was declared his passport was confiscated and he was bound not to leave the town until he returned to Berlin, his home where he had to get a permit to stay. On learning he was a journalist when he arrived at the English section of the permit department he was arrested and placed in a cell with two prisoners: one had been there a month, the other three weeks. It turned out there were many other English in the jail; they had been arrested at the British Consulate as they tried to find out how to leave. Eventually he was allowed to go home but told he had to report to his local police station every third day and stay in Berlin.

Restricted in his movements, he tried to continue his life which became increasingly more difficult and was made much worse by the inhuman conditions in Newbury Camp for German internees, as was reported in the German papers. When the liberal papers began to follow the right-wing press it was obvious to Cohen that change was afoot. When on 16 October the German government gave the British government an ultimatum about the release of German internees the next step was obvious. On 6 November, he was awoken and taken into internment along with many others.

One man, and there were probably others, had no choice but to stay before that right was taken away by internment. There were British men in German prisons serving sentences for crimes committed in Germany. One of them was Max Schultz, a Hull man convicted in November 1911 of spying. His release date had been set for 2.10pm on 13 June 1918.

The proactive internment of over 32,000 enemy aliens in Britain was to a large extent a response to xenophobia and coincided with outbreaks of anti-foreigner violence. It offered the state protection and it protected the enemy aliens from attack. In the initial stages the German approach was largely reactive and was directed by the state. While it could prevent spying and espionage the main reason for the German internment was in retaliation for the internment of its nationals in enemy countries. In mid-October, 'following reports of the systematic abuse of German civilians in British hands and allegations of spying and sabotage by enemy agents working inside Germany'[1] it was decided to immediately intern British males of military age. Against advice to have an internment camp well away from Berlin, it was decided to set up a camp at the racecourse at Ruhleben, just 2 kilometres west of the capital, between Spandau and Charlottenburg. Other camps were set up at Celle Castle, Havelberg, Holzminden and Rastatt. There were two camps at Holzminden – one camp for men and the other camp for women and children. The majority of the 10,000 internees were Belgian, French, Polish and Russian although there was a small number of British. Havelberg held 4,500 internees of various nationalities including British Indians.

Initially, Ruhleben was used 'to house Russian and Russian-Polish prisoners from the Berlin area … as well as a handful of Japanese citizens … after the Japanese entry into the war … A few Britons arrested as suspected spies or miscreants were also held there.'[2] In the four years it was open as a purely civilian camp, it housed 'some 5,500 Britons … with a population ranging from 4,273 in February 1915 to around 2,300 at the time of the armistice.'[3]

Although the literal translation of Ruhleben is 'quiet life', it was the most visited of all the German camps. It was also the most diverse: it contained men of all social classes and from across the empire; ordinary men, well-known men and men who would become known in later life. Among them there were black sailors, Grimsby fishermen, golfers, professional footballers, jockeys, drifters, conmen, thieves and stranded tourists. Some were pro-German and informed on the misdemeanours of others, some were married to Germans and some had been born in Germany. Ruhleben was truly international and included some whose countries were initially not at war with Germany. Cohen lists the following as being in the camp in the early days: 'Canada and South Africa, Australia and New Zealand, India, Jamaica and the Straits Settlements … Germany, Austria, and German Switzerland',[4] men who had been naturalised in Britain or colonies, 'including many who had neither seen England nor were able to speak a word of its language.'[5] The French group included 'Englishmen or naturalized Englishmen who had lived for very many years in Belgium or Northern France. And next came a motley group hailing from all corners of the globe – from Holland and Spain, from Finland and Mexico, from China and Arabia, from Poland and Ecuador, from Malta and the Cameroons.'[6]

As well as a mixed-bag of nationalities there were a considerable number of religions represented. While the majority were Anglicans, there were Non-Conformists, Roman Catholics, German Lutherans, Muslims, Hindus and Jews.

Among its already notable residents were Carl Fuchs (a celebrated cellist), Israel Cohen (a Zionist spokesman), Fred Pentland (ex-professional footballer and manager of the German Olympic football team), Steve Bloomer (ex-international footballer who was the newly appointed manager of Britannia Berlin 92) and Castle (a Transvaal Boer who, at 7 feet 6 inches tall, worked in a Berlin circus). Future notable inmates included Ernest Macmillan, George Merritt, John Balfour (later Sir John), Timothy Eden (later Sir) and Nico Jungmann.

There were also Ruhleben-only celebrities: 'Bambulai, the great Polish King' (an African who polished shoes), Peanut (a Cameroons-African who sold peanuts), *Naturmenschen* (who wore sandals and shaggy beards), 'a man of unbalanced mind who trampled about with a wet cloth on his bald head, sucking sweets and singing snatches of song; and a gentleman who always dressed as immaculately as if he were off to Regent Street – with well-creased trousers, fancy socks, resplendent tie, and monocle.' Popular characters included 'Lobster', a 'smart smiling youth who presided at the outfitting store, "Polly" and "Skinny" ... two men who took a conspicuous part as women in the dramatic performances.' 'Little Johnny' hawked the *Ruhleben Daily News*; there were two little Russian boys who had been captured serving as messengers; and there was an unsavoury character who boasted of having 'cycled from London to Monte Carlo, and who lent his mud-stained machine to his fellow-prisoners at a penny a ride.'[7]

A source of tension in the camp was drinking, particularly among the sailors who received money through the Mercantile Marine Association. Although banned in camp, it was brewed by the men and smuggled in by the guards and sold. While the drinking was mostly harmless, it did sometimes get out of hand and in June–July 1917 eight men were transferred to Havelberg camp for running around after nightfall, making a noise, disturbing the peace, and for the physical and verbal abuse of other prisoners.

Gambling was another banned activity, but this did stop some of the prisoners. Like alcohol, it was mostly a harmless pastime but for some it was serious and a number ran up huge debts.

The camp was home to 'a number of shady characters with previous convictions for theft, assault and other crimes, and one or two were in Germany in 1914 precisely because they were on the run from the British police.'[8] One barrack had a particularly bad reputation. Crossing anyone from it could result in a beating or having your face slashed.

There was no lack of skill in the camp, there was even a lion-tamer. The camp provided its own internal mailing system and produced its own stamps. The Germans also allowed the internees a printing press which they used to produce a camp magazine which was good enough to be praised by the highbrow *Strand Magazine*, who said the staff had 'every reason to be proud of their production'.[9] There was a French journal, *La Vie Française*, and an Italian periodical, *Il Messagero*.

Shops sold goods produced by the prisoners. Photography was a commercial activity leaving historians with a visual sense of the camp. Workshops taught a range of skills from book-binding to watch-mending, and on an intellectual level there were numerous classes providing knowledge in a wide range of subjects. Many languages were taught and the birth 'of professional and university courses through corre-spondence courses' is credited to Ruhleben.

Life in the camp was based around the barrack. The barrack was led by a barrack captain who represented the barracks, looked after internal discipline and oversaw the various sub-officials such as the cashier, fireman, laundryman and postman. Everyone was responsible for keeping the barracks clean but a levy could be used to pay someone else to do it. Wages were paid to men who undertook heavy labour or to those who undertook the more unpleasant jobs like cleaning latrines.

Conditions in the camp also created a free market where commodities were sold or traded. Men with money could pay for others to do their jobs or queue for them. Some of the inmates 'set up businesses offering hairdressing, tailoring, engraving or shoe mending services, all at competitive prices.'[10] Those with green fingers 'were allowed to cultivate small vegetable patches'[11] to supplement rations. A camp store sold articles from relief parcels and luxury goods were taxed. Any profits were 'used to pay for the police force, medicines, dentistry, stationary, cleaning utensils, funeral expenses and other essential items. The laundry and boiler-house were also "state-owned" enterprises and kept up a healthy surplus through the sale of passes and hot water for bathing and tea-making.'

Generally the camp ran smoothly and complaints investigated during and after the war were found to be baseless. Accounts were kept and scrutinised and found to be sound. Even the Germans were happy with the way the camp ran. When the camp commander was changed in 1916, he told the British camp commander that he had been told to keep things exactly as they were.

This did not mean that life in the camp was always satisfactory. Initially conditions were very bad but by the middle of 1915 improvements had been made to accommodation and washing facilities. The quality of food and medical care varied throughout the war as did the quantity of food which was reduced as the war went on. By the end of the war the internees were better fed than the local population, augmenting their ration with parcels from home.

Accommodation was a real problem at the start with six men to a horse box and 200 fitted into the sloping roof above the barrack, with little heating. Poor ventilation meant a stench-filled atmosphere. Crammed together with no electric light made life extremely unpleasant. The overcrowding was not solved until after a spate of early releases in 1918 when the population fell below 2,500.

The washing and toilet facilities were another problem. The camp was not set up to receive so many men and at the beginning there was one tap to about 300 men and no available hot water or mirrors. Fortunately most had brought soap with them as none was provided. A warm shower, interrupted by coal shortages, could be had once a fortnight, later reduced to a weekly wait. Cold showers could be taken at any time. The toilets were changed because they were seen as a health risk to not only the camp but Berlin as well. Their positioning at either end of the camp was inconvenient but saved the inmates from the epidemics that struck down many in PoW camps; 'there were no uncontrollable typhus, typhoid or cholera epidemics … caused by lice, contaminated water or unhygienic toilet facilities.'[12]

As in other camps the question of food, both quality and quantity, was always the most controversial. Initially prisoners relied on German rations which for a day consisted of poor quality bread, ersatz coffee, soup and blood sausage with skilly (oatmeal broth flavoured with meat). Dr Taylor, an American medical man, officially examined the rations provided. He stated that some of the food was bad and that 'the food provided and served during the week of the survey was not sufficient in any direction to provide nourishment … had they been entirely dependent on it.' [13]

The food improved after a corrupt contractor was removed and the camp took over the running of the kitchens. It was further helped by the arrival of food parcels from home. This coupled by improvements in dental and health care resulted in an overall death rate of just over 1 per cent, 'well below that experienced by military and civilian prisoners in other camps in Germany and elsewhere.'[14]

For the men in Ruhleben, like those in other camps, the main enemy was boredom. As in other camps the worst times were Christmas and the New Year. Boredom frayed tempers and there were occasional fights, and for those that could make or buy alcohol from somewhere, drunkenness. Like the thousands of other prisoners across Germany, the inmates took part in sports and any activity that took their mind off their captivity. Football teams were formed and games were played with fixtures planned weeks ahead. Football was stopped at one point because of the danger of broken windows. However, at the end of March 1915 half of the inner racecourse was given to the men for games of any type. This 'concession was granted by General von Kessel, the Commander-in-Chief of the Mark of Brandenburg, ostensibly in appreciation of the manner in which'[15] the camp was run. Naturally there was a sting in the tail: the rent for the field was £120 a year.

While football was the most popular sport, cricket and rugby also had their devotees. Between the close of the winter sports and the commencement of the cricket season, athletics completed the sporting calendar. Tennis courts, separated by nets, were laid out. So popular was the sport that courts had to be booked well in advance. The standard was high, as was the subscription, which excluded many men from the game. There were two players of note: J. O'Hara Murray and G.K. Logie, the latter an international player. The golf club, although restricted by the grounds, thrived and grew to about 200 members, many of whom were professional players. Other sports played included hockey, lacrosse, and baseball. There was of course boxing, gymnastics, weights, quoits, croquet, skittles and 'la pelote'.

Life in the camp was rich and diverse: the news-sheet, debating, theatre, orchestra, arts and science union, and many and diverse clubs. History was taught by John Masterson, later to be vice-chancellor of Oxford University and controller of the double-cross spy system during the Second World War; and Leigh Henry, who would later work for the BBC, lectured on a variety of subjects.

By autumn 1916 the camp school had a total of 1,400 students in 300 classes taught by 200 teachers of which nearly 70 were trained teachers; a few received a five marks honorarium for their work. 'The ages of the students ranged from 17 to 55, and father and son were often members of the same class.'[16] By the summer of 1916 many were working for the examinations of the Royal Society of Arts and the London Chamber of Commerce, as well as for the London Matriculation.

The twelve departments of the school were devoted to languages, science, commercial subjects, arts, music and handicrafts with tuition limited to small numbers to ensure individual attention. Most 'of the educational work was concentrated in the loft of Barrack VI.' It was portioned off to provide 'an office, lecture-room, twelve small class-rooms, and a laboratory'.[17] Classes were taught by well qualified teachers and classes included botany, agricultural, physical and inorganic chemistry, mathematics, engineering up to final year degree level, and numerous maritime courses that enabled the mariners in the camp to prepare for seafaring certificates up to the level of extra-master. The arts department ran courses in a wide range of subjects from Latin to drawing. Subjects such as commercial geography, book-keeping and shorthand were taught by the commercial department, while handicrafts taught included book-binding, wood-carving and fancy leather work. Mr E.L. Bainton, director of the Newcastle Conservatory of Music, presided over the department for Music where sixty students were enrolled for instrumental, vocal and theoretical work.

'Independent of the school, but supplementary to its activity, there were a large number of "Circles" which met to discuss original papers or addresses delivered by members. The French, German, Spanish and Italian Circles practised conversation and read together classics of the respective languages; while the other Circles were the historical, science, technical, engineering, nautical, banking, and social problems Circles.'[18] There were also literary and debating societies.

In July–August 1915 the latter group decided to hold a mock by-election. This was to ensure 'that the "borough of Ruhleben" was properly represented at Westminster.'[19] Three candidates stood for election: Alexander Boss (Conservative), Israel Cohen (Liberal) and Reuben Castang (Votes for Women). The two-week campaign, complete with committee rooms, posters and rowdy open-air meetings, parodied British elections. Mayor Walter Butterworth, as returning officer, declared Castang the winner. There were 74 spoilt votes making a valid vote total of 2,689, cast as follows:

Reuben Castang (Votes for Women) 1,220 (46.7%)
Israel Cohen (Liberal) 924 (35.3%)
Alexander Boss (Conservative) 471 (18.0%)

In PoW camps there was usually a shortage of books but Ruhleben was different. It ran a well-resourced reference library of 5,000 books sent from England. There was also a technical library and, most popular of all, the 'general lending library of about 6,000 novels, mostly in English, but also some in French and German.'[20] Like a regular library, it fined men who returned the books late.

As in every camp there was always a number of people who wanted to entertain others, be it in the barracks or on the stage. Ruhleben was no exception, and from rudimentary beginnings, theatre developed to become 'a permanent feature of camp life and a constant reminder of home'.[21] This was possible because of the talent available, in particular that of three men: John Roker (pre-war ballet master at the Metropol theatre in Berlin), Ernest Macmillan (composer), and Cyrus Brooks (lyricist). High-brow plays were performed alongside middle-brow thrillers, farces and Gilbert and Sullivan operettas. The most popular productions were those created by the prisoners, particularly pantomimes, especially as they were full of 'up-to-date references to the war and internment'.[22]

An important difference between a military PoW camp and a civilian camp were the inmates. Obviously they were civilian, a major difference, but also civilian camps contained 'PGs', pro-Germans. Why should some internees, locked up by the Germans, be anti-British? It was a simple confusion caused by place of birth or naturalisation. At the start of internment there had been in excess of 700 who were pro-German. Many were technically British subjects, but they had only remote or feeble ties with the country. 'For the most-part they were men who had been born and bred in Germany, who had acquired naturalisation after the minimum period of residence in England or one of her colonies, and who had returned to the Fatherland. They also included the sons and even grandsons of such naturalised Englishmen: men who had never set foot on English soil and were utter strangers to the English tongue.'[23] Others were English but had lived their lives in Germany and had little in common with their homeland. There were others of foreign birth who had also lived for the major part of their lives in Germany. All the groups had been surprised to be suddenly branded as enemy aliens when the war started. When the British PGs complained, they were bluntly reminded that they had hidden behind their nationality to escape military service and that they were free to join the army now.

As a level of animosity developed between the groups it became necessary to split them apart and in April 1915 separate barracks were created to solve the issue. Once isolated, the authorities tried to get them to enlist, which about 200 or so did, and of course they were struck off the British Relief Fund so received no help from Britain. Not all the PGs moved out when told to do so and they were slowly reintegrated into the British camp.

Like the men in PoW camps they could be repatriated if unfit for service and, like the soldiers, they were subject to medical examination and more often than not they were rejected. Cohen recounts that 100 were released in November and 150 in December 1915. Then numbers dropped and release became slow, release dates were put back and criteria changed. Only men over 55 could be certain of eventually being allowed home.

There were many who tried to escape from Ruhleben. Most failed, were caught and consequently punished. Walter Ellison was one of the successful ones. Already a camp hero for spending five weeks in detention for speaking out against German officers for using camp funds illegally, he made a home run in the autumn of 1917. It was his fifth attempt. He had previously spent nearly two years in Stadtvogtei, a civilian criminal prison, without any contact with the outside world for an escape attempt. This length of absence was not unique. William O'Sullivan Maloney spent over two years in Stadtvogtei and Havelberg before being returned to Ruhleben.

Although conditions were relatively good throughout, morale did decline and escape attempts increased during the latter part of the war. Most escapees were returned to camp to face solitary confinement but later in the war were transported to Havelberg after they had completed their detention at Stadtvogtei where conditions were much worse and relief parcels often restricted or denied.

The increasing numbers of men suffering nervous disorders was another sign of declining morale and some of the more serious cases had to be sent to the *Irrenanstalt* (lunatic asylum) at Neu Ruppin. This was reputed to be typical for the time with straitjackets and padded cells; a place from where men did not return or, if they did, they were 'mere shadows of their former selves'.

With the end approaching, many Ruhlebenites feared the worst: a revolution. Plans were made to defend the camp against hungry marauders who might break in to steal their food. It did not happen. There was a revolution, but it was milder than anticipated. On 4 November, a Kiel sailor who had befriended a Ruhleben mariner confirmed that the revolution had begun and then on 8 November a soldiers' council, formed of the guards, deposed their officers, lowered the flag and replaced it with a red flag supplied by some of the prisoners. Inmates were advised to stay in camp for their safety and that they would be released in a few days. Without guards, some naturally went into Berlin, most just to look but some went to sell their precious goods, 'soap and toothpaste',[24] and others to have a good time enjoying the plentiful alcohol and freely available women.

From 13 November the families of Berlin based internees were allowed to stay in the camp. 'Finally on 22 and 24 November a total of 1,500 prisoners and their families were allowed to proceed to Copenhagen'[25] and onwards to Hull or Leith. After a couple of days in reception centres they were allowed to make their way home. Some stayed behind because they were refused passports or because that is where they wanted to resume their lives. They had gone home but there were still over 24,000 Austrian and German civilian internees in Britain.

Ruhleben had been set up as a civilian internee camp but when it closed, after extensive looting by Germans, it suddenly had a new function. On 30 November, Russian PoWs from the Rhine area arrived to await their eventual repatriation to the Soviet Union.

Notes

1. Stibbe, M., *British Civilian Internees in Germany*.
2. Ibid.
3. Ibid.
4. Cohen, I., *The Ruhleben Prison Camp*.
5. Ibid.
6. Ibid.
7. Stibbe, M.
8. Stibbe, M.
9. Ibid.
10. Stibbe, M.
11. Ibid.
12. Ibid.
13. Stibbe, M.
14. Ibid.
15. Cohen, I.
16. Stibbe, M.
17. Ibid.
18. Ibid.
19. Ibid.
20. Stibbe, M.
21. Ibid.
22. Ibid.
23. Cohen, I.
24. Stibbe, M.
25. Ibid.

'Trafalgar Square' was the meeting point of the main streets in the camp.

'Bond Street' was one of the main thoroughfares in Ruhleben camp.

The captain of Ruhleben Camp and the camp council, from left to right: J. Powell, Captain Woolner, Captain Thomson, H. Redmayne and F. Bell.

Ruhleben theatre.

The camp was a converted racecourse. Much use was made of the grandstand to watch the world pass by and enjoy the sporting activities in the middle of the track.

The internees showed their love of gardening which kept them busy and also hid the fencing.

The laundry was set up as a business. These are the staff of Ruhleben laundry.

The military guard at Ruhleben.

The civilian police at Ruhleben.

Different nationalities did not mix very much in Ruhleben and certainly did not bunk in the same barracks. This picture shows members of the African barrack. The original photo is captioned 'the negroes barrack'.

Ruhleben contained a wide range of ethnic groups and races. On the left is the 'Boer Giant'.

The queue for dinner. Meals were picked up on an individual basis at Ruhleben.

A boxing bout in Ruhleben. As in the military camps, sport was always popular.

The majority of the internees in Ruhleben were English so cricket was a popular summer pastime.

The interior of the prison kitchen.

An orderly queue to pick up parcels.

The altar in Ruhleben church.   Ruhleben synagogue.

The military staff at Ruhleben at the start of the war. Left to right: Baron von Taube, Count von Schwerin (commandant), Rittmeister von Brocken and Count von Hochberg.

Many advanced educational courses were taught by highly qualified men. As with the art studio, they were able to build a science laboratory and perform experiments there.

Ruhleben orchestra.

The internees soon portioned off enough space to create an art studio.

A scene from a costumed musical production. With the severe shortages in Germany, the costumes are impressive.

A more leisurely game was chess, seen here being played outdoors during a hot spell.

A number of the Ruhleben men set up their own businesses, taking up where they left normal life.

Civilian internees continued to arrive throughout the war as a result of German naval activity. These are Hull and Grimsby seaman captured when their boats were sunk. The story of the trawler *Euclid* is typical. They had been attacked by a submarine, boarded, and the men taken prisoner and sent to Stadtvogtei, a pre-war civilian prison, before being sent to Ruhleben.

A photo of the cast of the October 1918 Ruhleben theatre production *Beauty and the Barge*.

ENGLÄNDERLAGER
RUHLEBEN · SPANDAU
GERMANY

XMAS 1914.

WISHING YOU A HAPPY XMAS
AND A BRIGHTER NEW YEAR

FROM

Albert Willy Josef

BRITISH CIVIL PRISONER OF WAR

ARMS & BADGES

OF

RUHLEBEN.

DUM SPIRO SPERO

1915.

SEAL OF THE BOROUGH
R D S

1916.

BRITISH CIVIL PRISONERS OF WAR
RUHLEBEN

POLICE

COOKS.

CAPTAIN BARRACK 2.

Concentration Camp for
British Civilian Prisoners of War.
Ruhleben, Germany.

Amusingly, a Christmas card from an inmate with a German name sent to German relatives in Germany. He was one of those British people that were actually German but were interned because they did not have German citizenship.

A postcard sent home by an inmate that attempts to sum up life humorously.

Chapter Six

Homecoming

To go home was what nearly all prisoners wanted and by November 1918 it was clear they might well be getting their wish. But at the same time there was an influenza pandemic sweeping the globe and many prisoners, weakened by their ordeal, succumbed. In his diary PoW Clarke recorded the death of one prisoner on 1 November 1918. Private Kelly, captured in September 1914, died from 'the Grippe', probably influenza, because the doctor was too late to help.

Those in the civilian internee camp at Ruhleben fared better than most PoWs, and indeed the civilian population. 'Between 3 and 18 July, out of a camp population of 2,336 men, some 1,565 cases of infection were reported. However, this resulted in two deaths only.'[1] This was achieved by closing off parts of the camp and stopping visits to the cinema and theatre. When compared to civilian deaths, at around 187,000, the number is remarkably low.

Many were to die in the last week of the war and before they could be released and transferred to Britain. The breakdown of the German transportation network meant that in many camps the parcels did not get through leaving prisoners weakened and more susceptible to infection. In October 1918 the camp at Quedlinburg was struck with typhus fever. It spread from the Russian to the French and finally the British compound, resulting in many deaths.

There were many reasons a man might be struck down, and the dying did not stop because there was an armistice. Among those returning should have been Rifleman Ambrose Bottomley, an employee at Fargas Oil Mills in Wincolmlee, Hull. He had been a PoW in Germany since October 1915 and his wife and three children looked forward to his arrival at any time. Early in the New Year they received notification that he would not return. After a short illness, he had died of heart failure on 17 November in Germany before he could be released.

Bill Easton, newly returned, found out that a local lad, also a PoW, was killed by a train in Germany while running to catch the train to take him home. Major Waite, 11th East Yorkshire Regiment, died on 31 January, shortly after release: he committed suicide. Some died on the short sea voyage home and more were to die in hospital. Others would die although they had been released from the army in a fit state. My paternal grandfather lost his best friend during the 1920s as a result of his suffering in Turkish PoW camp from 1915 to 1918.

Fortunately most would return home, the exception, in the short term, being the Russians. With Germany in turmoil and their own country now a different place to that they had left, what could be done to help them? Food was very short but there were large stocks of parcels intended for British PoWs who were now at home, so at least they could be fed for a while. The Germans wanted them out of the country but the British did not want them sent home because they might become Red Army soldiers. Eventually, to an uncertain future, they were put on trains and returned to Russia.

Although they warmly welcomed the armistice, released PoWs were not the first to arrive home. During 1915 men who could no longer fight had been exchanged for German PoWs but in 1916 this had been changed to internment in Switzerland. By the end of the war there were nearly 27,000 men of all nationalities residing there. For the British, along with all the obvious benefits of not being in a German camp, it meant that they could have visitors from home.

For men held working illegally in France or Germany and to those in camps near the borders of Germany the end was no surprise. To the men in camps deep in Germany and those in *Kommandos* it came as real news. The war was over and Germany had to 'release all prisoners of war immediately and without reciprocity'.

As it became obvious to the Germans that they were losing the war, some of the more aggressive guards and commandants toned down their behaviour. Many just quietly disappeared. For many prisoners, the news that they might go home soon came on 10 November, when prisoners were told that Germany had lost the war. Guards started to disappear in some camps, especially those who had been unpleasant to the prisoners, in others they remained.

At Münster Camp when the commandant addressed the assembled prisoners as 'Gentlemen' and not the usual '*Schweinhunde*', it was obvious the war was over. At Friedrichsfeld the interpreter asked them not to make too much noise when he informed them that Germany had lost the war. Prisoners in punishment cells were released and men were allowed to leave the camps.

In some camps the officers remained with reduced powers, in others they were stripped of rank. Roll calls still happened, or didn't. But in some of the eastern camps, like Preussengrube, despite the news it was to be work as usual. On 15 November, the Russian Poles were taken to the border and released to their own devices. But the British were kept at their work each day, with reduced hours. In some remote camps the news took over a week to reach them.

Some camps now ran out of food. Fortunately, prisoners had their parcels and some took pity on the plight of their erstwhile guards and gave them food. Such was the food shortage that civilians would go to the camps and beg for food.

As well as food, which was needed for the prisoners themselves, parcels contained luxuries which could be traded in towns. Corporal Speight, at Friedrichsfeld, who had given some of his food to the German corporal, was taken into town by the German with his mates, where, armed with a tin of cocoa or a couple of bars of soap, he would go to the local bars. In exchange for the goods, six men could drink all day. Because of his fluency in German he would not be released with his drinking comrades. He was kept behind as an interpreter until everyone else, including the sick being moved to hospitals, had left.

Men in France and Belgium, retreating with their captors, were simply told they could go home and abandoned. Their exit from the war was straightforward. Heading west to Allied lines they were befriended along the way by newly liberated villagers. Two train loads of prisoners were in Calais just four days after the armistice.

Many who had been working behind the lines suddenly found themselves billeted with the Germans – everyone was in the same fix, and according to Private Bellamy they 'generally got on reasonably well together ... it was almost as if four years of war had never been.'[2] Although they received no rations, food was provided for them by the Comité Nationale, a relief organisation, and the Belgians 'were free in their gifts'.[3] Having slept rough since their capture, few could resist the comforts of a bed and clean clothes so kindly offered by the locals. With all this available many decided not to travel but wait for the advancing armies to get them. For Private Bellamy it was just two weeks before the French arrived.

It was more difficult for those in Germany. Without guards, they could leave the camps at will, but where would they go? Some of those held close to the border headed home, but for most there was nothing to do but wait. It was to be a slow process because the Germans claimed not to have the transport available.

At Schweidnitz in Silesia, the revolution was ushered in without a single shot. The men in the local camp were to wait a month before they were taken home but it was not time lost. Captain Bennett wrote that they 'were not the unhappiest in our lives ... They were a prelude to a larger liberty – and our first opportunity of seeing anything of the life of the country at that time.'[4] The result of spare time, a wish to see the country, lots of goods to barter and no guards was naturally fraternisation. During their enforced stay many had picked up a few words of German, some were fluent. Some managed to become *persona grata* in German families and when the men from his camp assembled at the station for their departure to Danzig, 'the station yard was full of smiling inhabitants, many of whom had brought flowers, and they gave (the prisoners) a rousing cheer as'[5] they started on their long journey.

Not all the prisoners wanted to return. Men who had collaborated with the Germans viewed the prospect with misgiving as did those who had become habitual petty criminals in the camp. Private Preston at Langensalza camp recalled one man who had a very personal reason for not going home. He had worked on a farm and had had the freedom of movement others wished for. His reason for not going home was long but straightforward. 'Living in Manchester before the war, he had been a drop-out, very idle and no use to his family or society. But since he had been on the farm he had learnt all about sugar beet growing and general farming and now had the basis of a useful career. He had never been as happy in his life. He spoke quite openly of the fact that the farmer had to serve at the front and eventually he started sharing the farmer's bed with the farmer's wife. We understood his meaning and told him he could please himself, realizing that we would have our own problems to sort out after being away from home for five years.'[6]

Within days of the armistice being announced, questions were asked in Parliament. On 14 November the Marquess of Lansdowne asked Lord Newton, assistant Under-secretary of State for Foreign Affairs, what arrangements had been made or were being contemplated for bringing back the British prisoners of war. In reply Lord Newton told the house that 'arrangements have been made for the repatriation of prisoners from all the countries with which we have been recently at war. With regard to Austria, a certain number has already arrived in Italy or at Trieste, and the Earl of Cavan has been instructed, and the Italian Government have been requested, to take all the necessary steps to secure the early repatriation of such as desire or are entitled to return. With regard to Bulgaria, all the British prisoners, with the exception of, I believe, something between forty and fifty, are already in British hands. As regards Turkey, a considerable number of prisoners have already arrived in Egypt and other districts under our control. A certain number have also been exchanged across the lines, both in Mesopotamia and in Palestine. The bulk of the British prisoners in Turkey are concentrated in the neighbourhood of Salonika, and arrangements have been made to bring them from Salonika in British vessels. In the meanwhile the authorities in Egypt have been instructed to see that everything necessary for their comfort is supplied.

'As regards the prisoners in Germany, our information is that the number of prisoners who have arrived in Holland up to the present date are not believed to exceed, roughly speaking, 1,000. Our Minister at The Hague has appointed, with the approval of His Majesty's Government, a Committee consisting of the Consul-General at Rotterdam, our Military Attaché at The Hague, and General Bruce, who has himself been a prisoner in Germany, to act as a Committee charged with the welfare of our prisoners arriving in that country and their earliest possible repatri-ation. Extra medical supply and transport staffs are being sent out, and besides a very large stock of emergency parcels from the Central Prisoners of War Committee, 30,000 full kits and 30,000 rations for a month will be sent immediately as a first instalment. All Red Cross workers, VADs, and medical personnel now in Holland will be retained for the present to cope with the emergency if required. Besides such Dutch ships as may be available, seven ships capable of carrying 9,000 persons have been ordered to Holland to bring back the prisoners, and three of them sailed yester-day. I may add that, independently of these arrangements, a small party is expected in

England today or tomorrow. And I might observe, in connection with this, that the statements in the Press with regard to the arrival of British prisoners appear to be totally inaccurate.

'In addition to these arrangements, arrangements are being made in order to evacuate prisoners from the Baltic, if necessary, or from Copenhagen. In connection with these measures 10,000 kits and 10,000 rations for a month are being sent, and it is hoped to effect the repatriation of prisoners east of the Elbe by neutral ships from Baltic ports. For such of our prisoners as may return via Switzerland, like orders are being given. For these prisoners it is proposed to draw on the British Army in France for supplies of food, and a large supply of clothing has been placed at the disposal of General Hanbury Williams, our representative on the spot. For any prisoner who may be returned directly across the lines in France and Belgium, instructions are being sent to expedite their passage to the Channel Ports and to do everything possible for their comfort on the way.

'The whole question of moving the prisoners from the camps in Germany under the Armistice will be dealt with at an international conference which opens tomorrow [15 November] at Spa, at which Major-General Sir John Adye will represent the interests of British prisoners of war for some considerable time.'[7]

The apparatus for their return was in place. Lord Newton told the house what would happen on their arrival: 'All the combatant prisoners, on their arrival in England, will go to large reception camps, where it is to be hoped they will receive the heartiest of welcomes, their medical wants will be attended to, and arrangements will be made for giving them leave as soon as possible. Other arrangements are being made for the reception of the civilian prisoners. I trust and believe that, in so far as time allows, nothing will be lacking to secure that the practical gratitude of the nation shall be shown to those who have done so much and suffered so grievously in the cause of right.'[8]

One of those who would be returning home now the war was over was Max Schultz. Hull's spy had been released before the war ended but because of the dangerous situation in Germany it was safer in prison than out of it. True to his beliefs, in his days of relative freedom he had continued to spy, and, on his return on 26 November, reported to Military Intelligence. Sometime after this he returned to his family in Coltman Street to resume a normal life.

Hull, Dover and Leith, were selected as ports of return. The first steamers to arrive were the *Archangel* and the *Newport*, which brought home around 1,700 men. On their arrival, 'There was intense enthusiasm, the men shouting "Good old Blighty!" and "Back in civilisation again".' The King sent a message of welcome that evoked hearty cheers: 'The Queen joins me in welcoming you on your release from the miseries and hardships which you have endured with so much patience and courage ... We are thanked that this longed-for day has arrived, and that, back in the Old Country, you will be able once more to enjoy the happiness of home.'[9] By Christmas nearly 39,000 had arrived at the port of Hull and by the end of repatriation on 31 January 1919 the 'Home to Blighty', as it was affectionately known, had welcomed over 80,000 men on their return. Many of those returning received bread freshly baked by the residents of Freehold Street, who also distributed parcels from Peel House, the collecting point for PoW supplies in Hull.

The Times reported: 'British prisoners of war from Germany, numbering about 1,700, and including many from Holland, received a hearty welcome when they landed at the Continental riverside quay, Hull, this morning from the steamships *Archangel* and *Stockport*. Huge crowds gathered from early morning to greet the prisoners, and a small flight of aeroplanes circled over the ships as they were disembarked at 9.45. Major-General von Donop, in command of the Humber garrison, read the message from the King, which was received with great cheering. General von Donop said he would convey their response to the message to his Majesty. The police band played "See the Conquering Hero Comes," "Home, sweet Home," and "Auld Lang Syne" ... Complete arrangements had been made at Hull for the comfort of the men, by a band of women workers from Peel House, the depot for the sending of provisions to prisoners of war, and, in addition to refreshment, each man was handed a parcel of cigarettes, sweetmeats, and biscuits. The Lord Mayor was unable to be present, as he was attending a Thanksgiving service. The men, with the exception of a few belonging to Hull, were immediately taken by special train to Ripon Camp, whence they will be distributed to their homes. The address of the camp is:- Repatriated Prisoners of War Reception Camp, Ripon South. About 1,500 men arrived by the two boats, and two other boats will arrive to-day.'[10] Among arrivals two days later was Corporal Garforth VC who had been captured on 13 October 1914, less than two months after his arrival in France.

With the return of the men, relief organisations were wound up and took stock of what they had done. The table below is for Hull but can be taken as representative of the effort put in by volunteers to help local prisoners everywhere. The final total in today's money is around £3,000,000.

	1914/15	1915/16	1916/17	1917/19	Total		
Number of parcels (food and clothing) sent to PoWs	147	7,200	54,000	69,994	131,341		

	1914/15	1915/16	1916/17	1917/18	1918/19	Total £
Collected for PoW fund	0	1,960	10,862	27,951	14,855	55,628

Unfortunately repatriation, like release, was not as rapid as the men wanted. By December less than 10 per cent had reached England and by the middle of the month only half had reached Allied lines. Two months after the armistice there were still thousands of PoWs somewhere in Germany. To find them Red Cross units were sent to locate them. By the middle of February most were home.

The men left their camps, some having sold their parcels to the Germans, and proceeded to a designated port where they embarked for Britain. Those well enough to travel did so first. Those in need of medical attention were looked after until they had put on some weight and their health had improved. They too went home. Some instead went to a hospital in Britain for further treatment, but at least they were no longer a prisoner.

As relatives did not know when and where to find them, returning men could not meet their families until after dispersal from an army camp. They were initially met by crowds of well-wishers as their boat docked. Private Speight recalled what it felt like to be coming home. On board the LMS ferry *Londonderry*, they 'were all given a small flag and a bar of chocolate.'[11] When they entered the Humber they 'passed through lines of torpedo boats and drifters, all of which gave us a grand howl on their whistles. It made one's back hair curl to hear this rousing welcome.'[12] Even though they had been sent food in parcels he felt it necessary to comment on the food provided. It 'was a dream; bread and butter, tinned rabbit and bottles of stout at each meal.' He made no mention of a quayside welcome so perhaps by the time of his arrival interest in returning PoWs had waned.

Not all of the returning men were released from the army. 'Some were merely put through the inconvenience of returning to barracks for a week or two, others were asked to train new recruits or put older ones through their paces.'[13] Ernie Stevens was given the job of guarding German PoWs. At the dispersal camp they were showered, kitted out, examined and questioned about their experiences. It was generally an efficient process and most men went home in twenty-four hours, on two months' PoW leave to get their jobs back and with a gratuity from the government. While everyone was pleased by the homecoming not all the men received hugs and kisses, some were so different their families did not recognise them and could not respond appropriately to this stranger.

Many would fully recover and take up their old life but for a large number they would never be the same person again — mentally or physically. They were haunted by their experiences; some died young and some committed suicide. Many of those who had suffered the most did not get a pension. They had accepted a gratuity of £2 and signed a disclaimer that they were not suffering from any war-related disability. Why? Because to complete the necessary paperwork and be examined for a pension meant staying in the camp for another two or three days. They just wanted to go home.

The repatriation focused the attention of families whose loved ones had not returned and were still listed as missing. They drew some hope of resolution from the large numbers of newly-arrived PoWs. In just one edition of *The Hull Times* were thirteen requests for information. The following is typical: 'The parents of Private J.W. (Jack) Kirk, 11/51, 11th East Yorks, who reside in Knight Street, Barton, would be glad of any information concerning him. He was reported missing on March 27th last year, near Oppy Wood, and in spite of constant inquiries nothing further has been heard of him. It is thought some of the repatriated prisoners may be able to give some information.'[14] While some clung to hope, most realised that the missing would not return. Even by the time of the peace celebrations, there were still death notifications appearing in the press.

'The repatriation of French, Belgian, Italian, and Portuguese PoWs presented few logistical problems, once the necessary transport had been assembled. With the Russians, however, it was a different story.'[15] The process of exchange after Brest-Litovsk broke down with the German revolution, leaving hundreds of thousands of stranded Russians. With assistance from international Red Cross agencies many were transferred to camps in Britain and offered the chance to make a new life outside Russia. Many accepted; but many others elected to return to Russia, to an uncertain fate.

While at the camps the Germans were told they were going to pay for their behaviour, in reality little was done. The first trials were held in May 1921 and only nine Germans were prosecuted, seven for PoW offences. The cases tried were: Sergeant Karl Heynen, charged with mistreating British prisoners of war and sentenced to ten months in prison; Captain Emil Müller, charged with mistreating prisoners of war and sentenced to six months in prison; Private Robert Neumann, charged with mistreating prisoners of war and sentenced to six months in prison; Lieutenant General Karl Stenger and Major Benno Crusius, charged with mistreating French prisoners of war. Stenger was found not guilty, Crusius was sentenced to two years in prison; Lieutenant General Hans von Schack and Major General Benno Kruska, charged with mistreating prisoners of war, both found not guilty. It was no longer politically expedient to prosecute Germans for war crimes and the trials were quietly dropped.

Notes

1. Stibbe, M.
2. Jackson, R.
3. Ibid.
4. Ibid.
5. Ibid.
6. Jackson, R.
7. HL Deb 14 November 1918, vol. 32, cc90-3.
8. Ibid.
9. *The Illustrated London Life*, 1918.
10. *The Times*
11. Jackson, R.
12. Ibid.
13. van Emden, R.
14. *Hull Times*.
15. Jackson, R.

An exchanged British soldier pictured in England shortly after arrival.

Exchanged British soldiers on their arrival in Britain on 7 December 1915. A wonderful Christmas present for them and their loved ones.

British and French prisoners with nurses photographed during the examination process. After selection for possible exchange, the men were sent to Konstanz on the Swiss border where they were re-examined. The lucky ones were then taken across to Switzerland.

A cheering crowd of repatriated British prisoners aboard the SS *Archangel* arriving in Hull on 17 November 1918. Of the 1,700 men aboard the *Archangel* and the *Stockport*, some 900 belonged to the Royal Naval Division. 'There was intense enthusiasm, the men shouting "Good old Blighty!" and "Back in civilisation again".'

Missing Nine Months.

CAN any of our soldier readers at the Front throw any light on the fate of Pte. WILFRED GLEED, 1st Batt. Royal Berkshire Regt.? Last autumn he was officially reported missing on August 26, a date on which the Berkshires were retiring from Mons, and lost several men. No official news has reached his friends since, but a sergeant says that he fancied he saw Gleed fall as if shot and afterwards heard that he was removed to hospital. Information should be sent to Mr. and Mrs. Cotterell, 439, Oxford Road, Reading, uncle and aunt of Pte. Gleed.

PRIVATE WILFRED GLEED.

BUCKINGHAM PALACE

1918.

The Queen joins me in welcoming you on your release from the miseries & hardships, which you have endured with so much patience & courage.

During these many months of trial, the early rescue of our gallant Officers & Men from the cruelties of their captivity has been uppermost in our thoughts.

We are thankful that this longed for day has arrived, & that back in the old Country you will be able once more to enjoy the happiness of a home & to see good days among those who anxiously look for your return.

George R.I.

(*Left*) A newspaper appeal for information regarding a missing soldier. Unlike Sergeant Harrison he had not become a PoW, having died during the battle of Mons.

(*Right*) For their patience and courage PoWs were sent home with extra leave, back pay and later a letter from the King. In France they received a medal.

Not all the released soldiers were in the same condition. Many PoWs had not had access to their parcels, been badly treated or worked in very unpleasant and demanding conditions. Men like these did not go home immediately because they needed specialist care to recover.

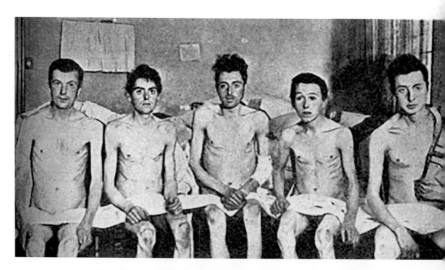

In the early days of the war some soldiers were exchanged through Holland.

Where this photo was taken is not known but it shows thousands of displaced Russian soldiers with their belongings just after the armistice.

Still dressed as prisoners, an early batch of returning British servicemen.

Men arriving home in December 1918.

A cartoon by Seaman Tooke about prisoner exchange. Death and escape were two ways to leave the camp permanently. The third was exchange, the best option but not an easy one. Usually only the most severe cases were guaranteed a return to the United Kingdom.

For those who were selected for exchange, this hotel in Switzerland was one possible destination. The picture shows the hotel and clinics at the Swiss town of Leysin.

Bibliography

Baer, C.S., *Der Völkerkrieg*, Volumes 1, 2 & 3, Julius Hoffmann, 1916.

Bilton, D., *Against Tommy*, Pen & Sword, 2016.

Bilton, D., *Hull in the Great War*, Pen & Sword, 2015.

Bilton, D., *Reading in the Great War*, Pen & Sword, 2016.

Bilton, D., *The Home Front in the Great War*, Pen & Sword, 2015.

Britannia.com, Prisoner of War, 2015.

Cohen, I., *The Ruhleben Prison Camp*, Metheun, 1917.

Crawford, O.G.S., *Said and Done: The Autobiography of an Archaeologist*, Weidenfeld and Nicolson, 1955.

Doegen, W., *Kriegegefangene Völker*, Verlag für Politik und Wirtschaft, 1921.

Durnford, H.G., M.C., M.A., *The Tunnellers of Holzminden*, Cambridge University Press, 1930.

Evans, A.J., *The Escaping Club*, Library Association, 1968.

Hall, M., *In Enemy Hands*, Tempus, 2002.

Hedin, S., *Ein Volk in Waffen*, Brockhaus, 1915.

Hedin, S., *Nach Osten*, Brockhaus, 1916.

Hinz, U. *Gefangen im Großen Krieg. Kriegsgefangenschaft in Deutschland 1914-1921*, 2006

House of Lords Debate 14 November 1918, Vol. 32, cc. 90-3.

http://encyclopedia.1914-1918-online.net/article/prisoners_of_war_germany

https://en.wikipedia.org/wiki/Holzminden_prisoner-of-war_camp

Hull Daily Mail, Various issues, 1914–18.

Hull Times, Various issues, 1918.

Jackson, R., *The Prisoners 1914–18*, Routledge, 1989.

Jones, Dr H., www.bl.uk/world-war-one/articles/prisoners-of-war

Lewis-Stempel, J., *The War behind the Wire*, Weidenfeld & Nicholson, 2014.

MacDonald, L., *To the Last Man*, Spring 1918, Viking, 1998.

Marks, T.P., *The Laughter Goes from Life*, William Kimber, 1977.

Middlebrook, M., *The Kaiser's Battle*, Allen Lane, 1978.

Moynihan, M., *Black Bread and Barbed Wire*, Leo Cooper, 1978.

National Park Service, *History and Legal Status of Prisoners of War*, 2015.

Reetz, W., *Eine Ganze Welt Gegen Uns*, Ullstein, 1934.

Rex, Hermann, *Der Weltkrieg in Seiner Rauhen Wirklichkeit*, Hermann Rutz, 1926.

Stibbe, M., *British Civilian Internees in Germany*, Manchester University Press, 2008.

The Illustrated London News, 1918.

The Times History of the War Volume VI, The Times, 1916.

The Times History of the War Volume XII, The Times, 1917.

van Emden, R., *Prisoners of the Kaiser*, Pen & Sword, 2000.

von Röper, Dr A., *Kriegsgefangene in Deutschland*, N.D.

Winchester, B., *Beyond the Tumult*, Allison & Busby, 1971.

www.historyextra.com/feature/forgotten-first-great-escape-1918

www.icrc.org/customary-ihl/eng/docs/v2_rul_rule25

www.northirishhorse.com.au

Index